PRENTICE-HALL
FOUNDATIONS OF CATHOLIC THEOLOGY SERIES

THE IMAGE OF GOD IN CREATION, by Sister M. Charles Borromeo Muckenhirn, CSC

THE WORD MADE FLESH, by David J. Bowman, SJ

SACRAMENTS OF INITIATION, by Henry J. D'Aoust, OSB

THE ONE GOD, by Wilfrid F. Dewan, CSP

CHRIST'S REDEMPTIVE SACRIFICE, by William F. Hogan

SIGNS OF TRANSFORMATION IN CHRIST, by John H. Miller, CSC

THE ISRAEL OF GOD, by John M. Oesterreicher

SACRAMENTS OF HEALING AND OF VOCATION, by Paul F. Palmer, SJ

ESCHATOLOGY, by John J. Quinn

THE CHURCH OF CHRIST, by Maurice Bonaventure Schepers, OP

THE THREE PERSONS IN ONE GOD, by Gerard S. Sloyan

THE LIFE OF GRACE, by P. Gregory Stevens, OSB

FOUNDATIONS OF CATHOLIC THEOLOGY SERIES
Gerard S. Sloyan, *Editor*

THE ISRAEL
OF GOD

On the Old Testament Roots
of the Church's Faith

JOHN M. OESTERREICHER

The Institute of Judaeo-Christian Studies
Seton Hall University
Newark, N.J.

PRENTICE-HALL, INC.
Englewood Cliffs, N.J.

Nihil obstat:

George W. Shea, STD
Censor Deputatus

Imprimatur:

✠ Thomas A. Boland, STD
Archbishop of Newark

July 9, 1963

Quotations from Holy Scripture follow in the main the Confraternity version. (© The Confraternity of Christian Doctrine, Washington 5, D.C.) Occasionally, however, the author has made his own translation. References to Scripture are frequently limited to one or two among many possible ones; others that will complement those given can easily be found by consulting the daily growing biblical literature. The author regrets that limitations of space forbid the listing of all biblical dictionaries, Old Testament theologies, and specialized books from which he has learned much of what he here offers to others. Though many remain unnamed, the author wishes to express his gratitude to a wide company of scholars who have not only eased his labors but largely made this study possible. Space requirements have also made it necessary to print part of the book in a smaller type than the main body. Such parts are essential, nonetheless, to the understanding of the whole.

PRENTICE-HALL INTERNATIONAL, INC., *London*
PRENTICE-HALL OF AUSTRALIA, PTY., LTD., *Sydney*
PRENTICE-HALL OF CANADA, LTD., *Toronto*
PRENTICE-HALL FRANCE S.A.R.L., *Paris*
PRENTICE-HALL OF INDIA PRIVATE LIMITED, *New Delhi*
PRENTICE-HALL OF JAPAN, INC., *Tokyo*
PRENTICE-HALL DE MEXICO, S.A., *Mexico City*

C

EDITOR'S NOTE

This series offers the depth and richness of the divine message of salvation proclaimed to us by Christ. The theology, or "faith seeking understanding," contained here is not on a catechetical level, nor yet on a complex, higher level; it is clear and nontechnical, but at the same time adult and thorough. It is a scholarly presentation of revelation.

These volumes do not adopt an apologetic approach. They neither attempt to justify Catholic faith nor aim at convincing those who do not profess it of the reasonableness of believing. This series is written primarily for those who already believe, who accept the Church as the living continuation of Christ, and the Scriptures as divinely inspired.

The authors do not attempt a philosophy of God or of Christianity, but a study of the mystery of God seen through the eyes of faith. The mystery of faith will not be dispelled by the study of these books. It will remain.

Since some background in philosophy on the part of the reader is needed, and cannot in every case be presumed, there are times when philosophical terms will need to be explained. Philosophical reasoning is very much a part of speculative theology.

Although the breakdown of the series is along traditional lines, each volume is designed to emphasize the oneness of God's plan of salvation and not its different facets. Distinction is made in order to unite. What is taught in the Scriptures is stressed, so that it may be seen how men of the Bible understood the message entrusted to them. The historical aspects of doctrine as held by Christians are then treated: the testimony of the early Christian writers and the liturgy to the belief of the Church; the controversies and heresies that necessitated defense and precise formulation, and finally, the magisterial teaching in each subject area. In this way speculative theology, or the present understanding of each mystery, is not seen in isolation from the sources of faith.

Thus, the revealed Christian message is viewed as the *tradition* (in the fullest and best sense of that theological term) expressed in and through the Church over the centuries—more explicitly formulated, from age to age, and with further applications. But it is still the same saving message begun in the Old Testament and perfected in the mystery and person of Jesus Christ.

One last point is important. Although the study of theology is an exercise of intellect, it can never be exclusively this. The message of Jesus Christ is a living Word, an invitation to participate in the saving event of the redemption, starting in this world by faith and the union of grace, and culminating in heaven by vision and immediate union. This invitation demands response or living faith. The study of the Christian message through theology requires such response, for the message is not something that was heard and assented to once. It is a Word addressed to us that requires our vigorous "Yes" for a lifetime.

CONTENTS

INTRODUCTION

PASCAL AND THE GOD OF ABRAHAM, *page 1*

Pascal's inner experience. Son of Abraham.

CHAPTER ONE

GOD, CREATION, MAN, *page 6*

THE GOD OF SCRIPTURE. *Religious experience and theological thought. The incomparable God. The Lord mirrored in his work. The living God. Yahweh: Mystery and Presence. The Holy One of Israel. The one God and his many names. The fatherhood of God.*

MAN IN CREATION. *Creation as prelude. A creature unto salvation. A creature of flesh. Man, the image. Man in his totality. The individual and the community; Israel and the nations.*

CHAPTER TWO

SIN, PARDON, REDEMPTION, *page 26*

THE GRAVITY OF SIN. *The horror of sin. The dimensions of sin. The universality of sin. The solidarity woven by sin.*

THE WONDER OF PARDON. *The open door of conversion. The penitential liturgies. The delight of the Forgiver.*

THE ABUNDANCE OF REDEMPTION. *The vocabulary of redemption: ransom; vindication. The theology of redemption. Jesus, Israel's and the nations' Go'el.*

CHAPTER THREE

COVENANT, GRACE, PEOPLE OF GOD, *page 46*

THE COVENANT OF PREDILECTION. *The sacredness of covenants. God's covenant with Israel. The law of descent.*

THE BOND OF GRACE. *The gratuity of grace. Grace ahead of man. Enduring love. The seeds of Christian teaching.*

GOD'S PEOPLE. *Chosen for others. The mediator people. Walking in his ways. Chanters before the Lord. Christ and the psalter.*

CHAPTER FOUR

KINGDOM OF PRIESTS, *page 63*

SACRIFICES. *God's presence. Atonement. The Suffering Servant.*

SACRAMENTS. *The nature of the sacraments of old. Circumcision. The soil of the Christian sacraments. Washings and baptism.*

PASSOVER: THE LAMB AND THE BREAD. *The meaning of the paschal lamb. The meaning of the unleavened breads. From family feast to national holiday. The solidarity of generations.*

CHAPTER FIVE

PROMISE OF NEWNESS, *page 77*

THE SIGNS OF NEWNESS. *A new exodus. A new covenant. A new David, a new Temple.*
THE NEW PASCHAL MEAL. *The universal pasch. The last supper: problem and solutions. The unfolding of the last supper. The significance of the last supper. The fruit of the last supper.*

CHAPTER SIX

DEATH, RESURRECTION, THE DAY OF YAHWEH, *page 93*

LIFE AFTER DEATH. *The enigmatic standstill of faith. The tyranny of death. The oppressiveness of the netherworld. First signs of hope. The heart's desire for lasting union. The final breakthrough.*
THE DAY OF YAHWEH. *Past and future victories. Judgment. Salvation.*

A FEW BASIC BOOKS, *page 111*

LIST OF ABBREVIATIONS, *page 112*

INDEX, *page 113*

INTRODUCTION

PASCAL AND THE GOD OF ABRAHAM

For two long hours on the evening of the twenty-third of November, 1654, an inner fire so filled the soul of Blaise Pascal that henceforth he knew only one passion: to live in and for Christ. Then in his thirties, this mystical experience found him at the fullness of his manhood and the height of his scientific pursuits.

When Pascal was only twelve years old, his father surprised him while he was attempting to solve a primary geometric problem. All by himself, he was trying to prove that the sum of the three angles of a triangle is the same as that of two right angles, apparently without knowing that he was working on the thirty-second theorem of Euclid. At the age of sixteen, he wrote a significant treatise on conic sections; at twenty, he constructed a calculating machine that for his day was as much a feat as the making of computers is today. In the years that followed, he shed light on the problem of vacuum and other scientific questions. Finally, when he was about thirty, he laid the foundations for integral calculus and thus became one of the pioneers of higher mathematics.

PASCAL'S INNER EXPERIENCE   The "night of fire" drove Pascal from the infinity of numbers to the infinity of the spirit. God's hand had touched him, had taken possession of his heart and burned on it the seal of love. Obviously, these are metaphors, but touch, taste, smell, sight, and sound are all we have to convey happenings that transcend the world of senses. Being an exact scientist, Pascal sought to retain by word and image that which was beyond word and image. As soon as he could, he recorded his experience on a piece of parchment in order to carry it with him always. Sewn inside the lining of his doublet, it was not discovered till after his death.

The *Mémorial,* as Pascal's document is called, is unique because it bears the freshness and immediacy that mark an experience untouched by later reflection. In an ecstatic stammer, it proclaims the unity between Old and New Testaments. Giving first the time and place of the grace-filled event, and thus snatching them from oblivion, the hastily written record continues:

Fire
God of Abraham, God of Isaac, God of Jacob
Not of the philosophers and scientists
Certitude, certitude, feeling, joy, peace
God of Jesus Christ
My God and your God
"Your God shall be my God"

The last exclamation is that of Ruth the Moabite on the way to Bethlehem, bespeaking her eagerness to come under the wings of the God of Israel. (Ru 1,16) The one preceding it is part of the comfort and the commission Jesus gave to Mary of Magdala in the garden of the resurrection. (Jn 20,17) Clearly, "*my* God and *your* God," "*your* God shall be *my* God" are far from neutral statements. They are intensely personal, for the God of Israel is not one of indifference: neither is he indifferent to man nor can man be indifferent to him.

It was God's love overflowing and hostile to neutrality, which Scripture calls his "jealousy" (Dt 5,9; Jos 24,19), that made Pascal utter his firm "No!" to the "God of philosophers and scientists." There was no contempt for philosophy or science in his protest, only an acknowledgment of their limits. For Plato, God holds the beginning, the middle, and the end of all things existing, while man is, at best, a plaything, a puppet of God. Or must one say a puppet of the

2

gods? (*Laws*, IV,715E; I,644E; VII,804AB) [1] For Aristotle, God is the first principle, the unmoved mover—unmoved, that is, in a twofold sense: He is the origin of movement; his perfection, however, does not seem to permit concern with the affairs of men. (*Metaphysics*, XII, 7, 1072^b 19-20; 8, 1073^a 25; 9, 1074^b 15—1075^a 10) Such is not the God of Scripture. He, the infinite One, has chosen man—no more than a speck when compared even to the smallest of stars—as his partner. The Lord keeps him in his thought; the everlasting eyes rest on him. (Ps 8,5)

When a scientist tries to read the Creator's blueprint, he may discover designs and laws, he may follow the line that leads from cause to effect, or he may detect spontaneous events. Still, if he remains immured in his laboratory, he will never see what only faith can see, that it is "love which moves the sun and other stars." (Dante, *Paradiso*, 33,145) Architect, director of the world's stage, first principle, and prime mover are certainly not meaningless titles for God. The God who invaded Pascal's life, however, was infinitely more: He came like "a thief in the night." (1 Thes 5,2) Strange thief was he; having taken some odds and ends, he left behind a new life.

The word fire that heads Pascal's *Mémorial* refers not only to the newly won ardor of his heart but more so to him whom Scripture calls "a consuming fire." (Dt 4,24; Heb 12,29) A fiery torch was God's signature to the covenant he concluded with Abraham. (Gn 15,17) Out of a bush burning but not burnt, the imperishable and ever-present One spoke to Moses. (Ex 3,2) When promulgating the commandments, which map out man's moral ascent, the majesty of the Lord descended upon Mount Sinai in sheets of flame. (Ex 19,18) Belief in Jesus will plunge men into the life of the Spirit and into a sea of fire, the Baptist prophesied. (Mt 3,11) To burn away evil as with a searing iron, to ignite the earth with his love, was and is Christ's wish. (Lk 12,49) At Pentecost, the Spirit both hid and manifested himself in flashes of light and tongues of fire. (Ac 2,3) "Fire," then, is one of the divine names. The true God yields to no contender, he demands man's entire being: The creature's total existence is his domain.

"Fire" is not the only divine name the *Mémorial* invokes. In the depths of his being, Pascal felt the presence of the God of Abraham, Isaac, and Jacob: the God who speaks to man and acts on his behalf; the God whose words are deeds, and whose deeds words; the "God of the Amen," that is, of fidelity and trust (Is 65,16); the One who stands by his promise and carries out his saving design. A hope-filled future, such is his plan for Israel, and thus for the world: weal, not woe; peace, not evil; salvation, not doom. (Jer 29,11) Through his predilection for the patriarchs, he made known his partiality for man. Through mighty and awesome deeds (Dt 10,21), he shaped Abraham's descendants into a people. Not by the round of seasons was Israel taught the meaning of her exist-

---

[1] In Plato, a philosophical approach exists side by side with the colorful fantasies of Greek mythology. As a religious man, he speaks the language of the poets before and the people about him; as philosopher, he is a genuine theistic thinker. On the one hand, he anticipates the classical proofs of God's existence (*Laws*, X,884–912) and insists that God is good, incapable of falsehood or deception. (*Republic*, II,379A–383D) On the other hand, the gods take care of matters great and small; they are our allies against evil (*Laws*, X,900–901; 906A), and yet we are said to be their puppets.

ence, and that of all men, but by sacred events. It was, then, in the light of redemptive history whose heart is the *magnalia Dei,* the great things God has done in Christ (Ac 2,11), that Pascal saw the meaning of his life as he never had before.

SON OF ABRAHAM   In a flash of the Spirit, Pascal saw himself as an off-spring of Abraham, the man of faith. Through Christ, he had been made a son of the living God, of the God whom both Testaments call the God of Abraham, Isaac, and Jacob. (Ex 3,6.16; Mk 12,26f; Ac 3,13)[2] It was the God of Abraham, Isaac, and Jacob who delivered Israel from the bondage of darkness; it was the God of Abraham, Isaac, and Jacob who freed his Servant Jesus from the bond-age of death. It was the same God who freed Pascal from a spirituality that was largely routine and filled him instead with a wholeness of being only he can give. In that night inflamed by love, Blaise Pascal, the great mathematician, re-alized that greater than the gift of genius was the gift that had made him a branch of an undying tree—the tree whose roots are in the Israel of old.

Unique and personal though Pascal's experience was, its contents had always been part of the Church's deposit of faith. What he saw corresponded fully to the Church's vision of herself as the spiritual continuation of the ancient Israel. At the Easter Vigil, when blessing the baptismal font, the new Israel rejoices in the old Israel's safe crossing of the Sea of Reeds and her rescue from the on-slaught of her pursuers as an anticipation and image of baptism. In the second collect, the Church prays:

> O God, we see your miracles of old shine anew in our own day. The salvation your mighty arm once wrought by freeing the one peo-ple from the persecution of Egypt, your arm now accomplishes for the gentiles in the waters of rebirth. Grant that the world in its full-ness pass over to the sonship of Abraham and share in the dignity of Israel. Through our Lord Jesus Christ.

The entire liturgy, particularly the prayers that are part of the administra-tion of sacraments, is replete with manifestations of this living link between the two covenants. To give only a few instances: Before an adult is baptized, the Church pleads with God that, as the Israelites were guarded on their march through the desert by an angel of his covenant love, so may the catechumen be. At the beginning of every Nuptial Mass, the Church begs that the God of Israel be ever with the newlyweds. Later in the Mass, she expresses her trust that the virtues of Rachel, Rebecca, and Sara, the holy women of old, be those of the bride. Heaven, God's infinite presence and life in his presence—life that is never-ending vision, never-ending love, and thus never-ending joy—she calls, at the burial of each of her children, "Abraham's bosom."

When blessing a house, the Church sees it as a duplication of the tent where God visited Abraham, where Isaac was born, where Jacob bowed for his father's blessing, in short, the tent where the history of salvation began. Seeds and seedlings remind her of the first fruits the children of Israel were told to offer. To her faith, arching the ages, organ music takes up the praise the sons

4

---

[2] A period between verse numbers indicates that the verses cited are successive but nonconsecutive.

of Israel sang to God with trumpets and cymbals. For her, the bells in her towers echo the sweet tunes of David's harp and the threatening thunder that dispersed the enemies of the chosen people. Finally, she would not consecrate a bishop, did he not first profess that the Author of the Law, the Prophets, and the Apostolic Writings is one, God the almighty Lord.

These visions of oneness, of progress from the old to the new, are not the futile reminiscences of old age. On the contrary, they are potent signs of the Church's youth. A Christian who is unaware of the unity of God's saving design cannot realize that his faith is the ripe fruit of many generations; he cannot appreciate that his redemption is God's work prepared for century upon century. Unaware of this wonder of growth, a man would be as if lost in a world of unrelated eras, though in reality he lives in a universe whose ages are lovingly ordained one to the other.

The purpose of this book is to give an idea of the kinship that binds together the Ancient and the New Dispensations. Though the limitations of space do not permit either a complete treatment or always a genetic one that would show the growth of each tenet of faith, the instances presented should shed sufficient light on the Old Covenant as the vital background of the Catholic creed and life. This is not meant as a piece of oratory. The biblical setting is an organic part of the Church. As the Old Testament beginnings of faith and life came to their consummation in the New, they were not all discarded. In some instances their realities, in others the inner secret of those realities, live on among the people of God remade so as to encompass Jews and gentiles, so as to cover the earth. (Eph 2,14; Mt 28,19; Rom 10,18) It is this blessed continuity that makes St. Paul call the Church "the Israel of God." (Gal 6,16)

CHAPTER ONE

GOD, CREATION, MAN

To reason that God exists is one of the great exploits of the human mind. In proving that he is more than an idea, more than a moral postulate, more than an imaginary construct, more than a shadow begotten by fear, the mind acts like a sovereign and yet like a servant—sovereign of the world it beholds and servant of the One who beholds world and mind. In proving that God is, the mind bends, with the rest of creation, before him who sustains and moves the entire universe.

THE GOD OF SCRIPTURE

Strange though it may seem to us, heirs of a long and honored philosophical tradition, the Hebrew men of old did not engage in metaphysical inquiries. It never occurred to them to approach God by way of elaborate reflection. *God was.* He himself had proved it by his great and gracious deeds, and this was all the certainty they desired. Only one lone passage in the book of Wisdom, which was written in Greek around 50 B.C., gives attention to the "discovery" of God by the discursive process from premise to conclusion. To its writer, ignorance of God is bottomless folly. To see the good about us, and not know him who *is;* to contemplate the works, and not find their Maker; to be enraptured by the splendor of creation, and not ascend to the Author of all created beauty is to be hollow. (Wis 13,1–9)

RELIGIOUS EXPERIENCE AND THEOLOGICAL THOUGHT   With the exception of this one chapter of Wisdom, rational proofs of God's existence are absent from the Old Testament. Biblical man had as little need for them as a child in his father's arms has for a scientific demonstration that the arms are alive. Unlike other nations, Israel came to know God through a spiritual encounter: through revelation. Having experienced—at the time of her delivery from Egypt and many times thereafter—his strong hand, his might and care (Dt 11,2; Os 11,3), she required no further evidence. Unconcerned with philosophical speculation and formal arrangement of the divine teaching, the biblical writers attempted no systematic treatise on God. No enumeration of attributes could do justice to him whom "the heaven of heavens cannot contain" (2 Chr 2,6), whom no earthly concept could encompass.

Still, theologians have sought, and will forever seek, to arrange in a systematic order God's revelation throughout sacred history. A theologian who obeys this impulse toward a firm hold on God's word carries out a needful and noble mission. True, all human efforts to interpret the divine mystery are inadequate. Even if a theologian does well, he does poorly. Even if his reasoning is that of a genius and his speech that of a poet, his work will be no more than a stammer. But stammer he must, not to make God his prisoner, but to make himself God's captive.

THE INCOMPARABLE GOD   According to the Second Isaia, it is absurd to represent God by a man-made figure. (Is 40,18ff) Shortly before venting his sarcasm on those befooled by idols, however, the prophet himself is compelled to resort to images from the world of man. He sees no other way of bringing out the Lord's peerlessness, his infinity, than to portray him as a giant. In fashioning the universe, God cupped the waters, as it were, in the hollow of his hand, marked off the heavens with a span, weighed the mountains with a scale and the hills with a balance. (Is 40,12) The paradox of comparing the incomparable runs through the whole of Scripture. It could not be otherwise. In making human language the vehicle of his revelation, God made the entire realm of analogy, metaphor, similitude, and image his medium.

Osea offers a striking example. To assure his hearers that the divine love they had spurned would in the end be triumphant, he had the Lord declare that he was God, not man, and thus would not carry his seething anger to the point of destruction. Rather would he roar like a lion so that even those afar would hear his voice and return home. (Os 11,9ff) When Israel kept multiplying and multiplying her infidelities, the prophet had to announce punishment: as a panther lurks by the road, so the Lord would watch for them; with the fury of a bear robbed of its cubs would he rend his people. (Os 13,7f) Such, however, was not the final judgment. There would come a day when he would forgive their guilt and show them mercy, when he would heal them with his love and refresh them as the dew does the field. (Os 14,2–6) Lion, panther, bear, even the dew of the field serve as the semblance of him who has no created semblance.

Despite the emphatic disclaimer by the book of Job that God has eyes of flesh to see as men see (Jb 10,4), many biblical writers speak of God's eyes. They mean, of course, his watchful omniscience—man's comfort or terror. (Prv 15,3; Am 9,4; Ps 10[11]4) Without the least embarrassment, they refer to God's arms, hands, fingers, and feet; to his face, mouth, lips, and nostrils; even to his back. To expound only two of these terms, God's arms and hands point to the power that created the world, directed Israel's history, and protected his people. Beneath his arm there is safety. The man upon whom his "good hand" rests prospers in his undertakings and accomplishes what he set out to do. (Esd 7,9) The arm of God does still greater things. Once his "holy arm" is bared, salvation comes to all the ends of the earth. (Is 52,10) Again, God's face means his presence—the people's guidance and support, their rescue by his love and pity. (Is 63,9) "To seek his face" is to seek him, to long for the manifestation of his life-giving grace. When "he hides his face," he turns from man's sin in "anger"; when "he lets his face shine," he shows his good favor. (Pss 103[104]29; 30[31]17)

Untroubled by the simplicity—some think the crudeness—of such anthropomorphisms, the inspired writer has God walk in the garden as the daily breeze cools the air (Gn 3,8); shut the door of the ark after Noa, his family, and his animals have entered (Gn 7,16); come down to see the city of Babel and the tower the *hýbris* of its inhabitants has built. (Gn 11,5) Not only were the authors of these and similar passages untroubled, they seem to have taken delight in narratives that depict God as having the shape, manner, and feelings of a man. How is this possible since the whole of Scripture proclaims God as the transcendent One, above time and space, unbound by the limits of tribe, people, province, and empire? How is it possible that the singer of one psalm passionately declares that Israel's Guardian neither slumbers nor sleeps (Ps 120[121]4), while the singer of another cries out:

8

> Awake! Why are you asleep, O Lord?
> Arise! Cast us not off forever!
> (Ps 43[44]24)

Might it be that God's infinite richness, his incomparability cannot be grasped, even tenuously, except by opposites? He is ever at rest and ever at work; he is all stern and all gentle; he dwells in light inaccessible (1 Tm 6,16) and yet he is near those who cleave to him in prayer and right doing. (Dt 4,6f)

THE LORD MIRRORED IN HIS WORK   Another of these opposites might clarify still further the subtlety of anthropomorphisms and anthropopathisms which, though less favored in later writings of Scripture, are never absent from its pages. The biblical doctrine about God is unmistakable: He is not a human being that he should change his mind, not a man that he should repent his deeds. (Nm 23,19; 1 Sm 15,29) Yet, in the story of the flood we are told: "When the Lord saw that the wickedness of man on the earth was great, and that man's every thought and all the inclination of his heart were only evil, he regretted that he had made man on the earth and was grieved to the heart." (Gn 6,5f) At first glance, this sentence seems to bring God down to our level. In reality, it exalts him as much as human words can. For it attributes to him not the petty feelings many pagan myths ascribe to their gods, but the strong emotions of a lover. True, nothing could be more human than to say, as does the inspired writer, that having had to watch the betrayal by his favorite creature, the Lord regretted having wasted his tenderness; that the heart of God was riven because his affection had been ignored and his gift scattered to the winds. Nothing could be more human and, at the same time, more divine.

What the introductory sentence to the flood story wishes to convey is that the Lord has not withdrawn from his creation. He is not an absent God. Rather does he love all things that are and loathe nothing he has made; he, the Master, is the friend of life, and his "imperishable spirit is in all things." (Wis 11,24.26–12,1) Man is especially dear to him: Without ceasing does he pursue the people he has made his own; the nations, too, are not far from his care. To none does he deny his blessing. There will be a day when enemies will be intimates, when the Egyptians will be called his people and the Assyrians the work of his hands, when both will live in harmony with Israel his inheritance. (Is 19,25)

The reason, then, for anthropomorphisms is obvious. Man—every man of whatever century, land, and culture—cannot enter the realm of the spirit except through the door of the senses. To no other people was this approach as self-evident as it was to the ancient Hebrews. Far from disdaining the world seen, heard, smelled, tasted, or touched, they valued it as the abode of the word and thus the parable of things divine. In one of the great songs of Scripture, bearing Moses' name, the community of Israel is warned not to forget what it owes to the Lord. The singer knew no better way of describing God's work than the use of metaphors taken from nature, that mirror of uncreated wisdom and wonder of cooperation among creatures. Like "the apple of his eye," the inspired poet told Israel, the Lord has guarded her. In rescuing her from Egypt, he acted like an eagle which incites its nestlings into flight, which spreads its wings be-

9

neath them so that they would not be dashed to the ground, which bears them up on its pinions. (Dt 32,10f)

There is a straight road from the Old Testament at-homeness in the world of sound, color, and fragrance, to the parables and sacraments of Jesus. In the parables, a dutiful farmer, a daring merchant, a tired woman, and a quick shepherd—with the help of seed, pearl, coin, and sheep—act out the drama of God's dealings with men. In the sacraments, things of everyday life—water, oil, bread, and wine—are turned into instruments of grace; they are God's assistants in the work of sanctifying man, and man's helpers in the business of glorifying God.

THE LIVING GOD   In his generosity, Israel's God summons his creatures to give him their support, though it is only by his support that they are and move. He has nothing in common with the gods of the nations—those things of nought, those powerless nonentities. (Jer 2,5; 1 Chr 16,26) At all times does his power keep and sustain the world. He has nothing in common with the fertility gods of Israel's neighbors. Like the seasons, they come and go, vanish and return, while he is ever the same, without beginning or end. He has nothing in common with pagan idols, which are like corpses hurled into the dark. (Bar 6,70) The God of Israel *lives*. Indeed, one of the oldest and most expressive names given him throughout Scripture is "the living God."

The Lord is the fount of life. Not only does he bestow life on man (Nm 27,16), all that lives lives by virtue of his spirit, his creative breath.[1] In particular is he the source of the extraordinary, as well as the ordinary, forms of human activity. Samson's strength, like all vital energy, came from God. (Jgs 14,6) The skill of artists is his gift. (Ex 28,3) It is "the breath of the Almighty" that grants insight to the wise and confers understanding of what is right. (Jb 32,8f) No less is rapture the work of the life-giving spirit; it makes a man a prophet, "another man"—a man of God. (1 Sm 10,6f) These singular gifts are small when compared to the all-imbuing life the faithful Israelite, through God's grace, called his own. It entered every level of his existence. Thus the frequent cry that the Lord may give life:

---

[1] Because God is the Author of life, life was sacred to the ancient Hebrews, and so was blood, the seat and symbol of life. Woe to him, went the saying, who sheds the blood of his fellow; from the ground it cries to God for vengeance. (Gn 4,11; 9,6) Even the blood of animals merited respect; hence the Old Testament enjoined: "Blood you shall not eat." (Gn 9,4) Its true use was cultic. (Lv 3,17; 17,10ff) Again because God is the Lord of life, prosperity was considered a blessing. He promised his people a land where they would be able to eat without stint, lacking nothing; yet he threatened that earthly goods would remain theirs only if they were mindful of their Giver. (Dt 8,6–20) If anyone thinks that the early Hebrew idea of prosperity as a token of divine pleasure was a form of materialism, he betrays little historic sense and little spirituality as well. Voluntary poverty as a virtue is not genuine without esteem for those goods of creation which the ascetic man has sacrificed for the sake of still greater goods. The "wealth" the Israelites of later days longed for was "to sit under one's vine and fig tree" (1 Kgs 4,25; Mi 4,4; Za 3,10; 1 Mc 14,12), a proverb expressing the ideal of a life on the land, moderate and calm.

the life begotten by his word and received by his promise, the life permitting his praise and dispensing light as well as joy.[2] Great is his quickening power, for thus says he who is high, exalted, and eternal, the Holy One:

> On high I dwell, and in holiness,
>   and with the crushed and dejected in spirit,
> To revive the spirit of the dejected,
>   to revive the hearts of the crushed.
> (Is 57,15)

One of the oldest and most solemn formulae of oath-taking in ancient Israel was *chai Yahweh*, a phrase so crisp that translators have tried to bring out its force in various ways. "By the life of Yahweh," "As surely as the Lord lives," "The Lord lives," are some of their renderings. Similarly, God was made to seal his threats and promises by the exclamation: "As I live," or "Forever I live." "The Lord lives" could serve as a pledge only because these words compressed Israel's entire spiritual experience. They were a creed, a succinct profession of her faith. "The living God" is the only God. He is the Guarantor of truth and justice whose will cannot be flouted with impunity. (Nm 14,21ff) He is the true God who endures forever. (Jer 10,10; Dn 6,27) He was at Israel's side, fighting with his people, leading them in battle, dwelling in their midst, guarding them against their enemies and against themselves, thus making them safe and setting them right. (Jos 3,10; 1 Sm 17,26; Ps 17[18]33–37.40f) The devout man thirsted, his heart and flesh cried out, for the living God, whom to approach is happiness, whom to find is salvation. (Pss 41[42]3.7; 83[84]3.5)

Few titles, then, were dearer to faithful Israelites than "sons of the living God." (Os 2,1) Preeminently, this title belongs to the One who, true to his mission from the first to the last, was the well-beloved of his Father. "You are the Messia, the Son of the living God," Peter professed while he still walked with him. (Mt 16,16) Later, after Jesus had risen, he climaxed his faith by speaking of him as the "Prince of life," the One leading his followers to the abundance which is his own, indeed, sharing it with them. (Ac 3,15)

YAHWEH: MYSTERY AND PRESENCE   With the French exegete Father Jacques Guillet, we may say that the appellation "the living God" expresses perfectly the experience granted man

> in the sight of Yahweh: that of an extraordinarily active presence, of an immediate and total spontaneity, which grows neither weary nor listless (Is 40,28), which neither slumbers nor sleeps. (Ps 120 [121]4) The Lord's language at Horeb, at the very moment he reveals his name, well conveys this intensity of life, this attention given to his work: "*I have witnessed the affliction of my people,*" he says

II

---

[2] Pss 118[119]25.50; 79[80]19; 35[36]10; 15[16]11.

to Moses, "*I have heard* their cry . . . *I know* well what they are suffering. Therefore *I have come down* to rescue them. . . . *I will send·* you to Pharao. . . ." (Ex 3,7–10) The "I am," for which these divine outbursts prepare, can hardly be less dynamic than they are. (X. Léon-Dufour *et al.*, eds., *Vocabulaire de théologie biblique* [Paris: Les Editions du Cerf, 1962], col. 219)

The "I am" in Guillet's passage refers to the mysterious utterance that came to Moses from the heart of a flaming bush. Frightened by the commission to take his people out of Egypt, Moses wondered by what name he should call God when standing before his oppressed brethren. *Ehyeh asher ehyeh,* "I am who I am," was the answer granted him. (Ex 3,14) No words could be simpler, yet they are so brimful of meaning that they admit of several interpretations, the most important of which are two. The choice of interpretation depends on how one understands Moses' question, and the meaning of his question depends on what he expected his people to ask for. Was it the assurance that God's power would be with them? Or was it the knowledge of God's innermost name that—according to pagan belief to which they had been exposed for so long—would give them power over him? In the latter case, the divine answer would have to be understood in terms like these: "I am who I am: the Inscrutable, the Ineffable. None can seize my name—the secret of my being—and thus win power over me. Unlike idols, I cannot be manipulated. Only those who trust and obey me will taste my strength." In the former case, the divine revelation may read like this: "I shall be who I shall be: your Deliverer, your ever-present Ally. I shall be at your side always, to rescue and uphold you. Depend on me. Trust and obey, and you will have my almighty support."

These interpretations do not necessarily exclude one another. If the two are combined, the words *ehyeh asher ehyeh*—from which the book of Exodus derives "Yahweh," God's proper name—are indeed a divine self-disclosure. This, then, would be the revelation that burst forth from the flames: Mysterious though the Lord is, he is never far. He is the compassionate Listener to Israel's woes and the merciful Champion of her redemption. Yet he remains impenetrable, even in his pity. His presence, ungovernable by man, is a saving one. Thus his will toward Israel's and mankind's salvation is immutable, not because he is beholden to man but because he is the One he is: Yahweh, the living, loving, holy God.

THE HOLY ONE OF ISRAEL   When Scripture proclaims God as living, loving, and holy, these adjectives must not be taken in their common significance. There is in them a breadth and totality, an inward ardor and irresistible power unknown among men. The God who is life sends rebels to their death (Ex 32,26–35), the God who is love wreaks his anger upon sinners (Jer 4,4), and the God who is holiness consumes the arrogant, as a fire does a forest. (Is 10,12–19)

12

I am Yahweh, this is my name;
my glory I give to no other.
(Is 42,8)

Ruling the events of men, he summons all generations from the beginning of time so that the prophet can say in his name that Yahweh is the first, and with the last he will always be. (Is 41,4)

As Moses walked curiously toward the burning bush, he was bidden to halt and remove his sandals. Only barefoot, freed of self-reliance and pretense, was he allowed to approach the flaming mystery. Even though the Lord was hidden from sight by a living torch of many branches, Moses covered his face. (Ex 3,5f) Whatever the imperfections of the Old Testament may be, from the first page to the last it is pervaded by a sense of the infinite distance that separates man from God, even the holiest of men from the Holy One of Israel. In the presence of him who sees but cannot be seen, Abraham was assailed by the darkness of fear, Jacob shuddered, while Daniel felt his strength ebbing till he fainted. (Gn 15,12; 28,17; Dn 10,8) Before him, august and majestic, Abraham trembled: "I am but dust and ashes," Isaia cried out: "I am lost, I am undone," while Job professed his insignificance, his nothingness. (Gn 18,27; Is 6,5; Jb 40,4) Because the Lord is holy, the earth quakes, the people tremble, and the faithful worship prostrate at his footstool: He reigns as King, high above, great, awesome, mighty, and just. (Ps 98[99]1–5)

Whereas sin defies his eyes of glory (Is 3,8), faith blesses the Lord. It pays the honor due him and acknowledges him as the One he is: the absolute and transcendent God, full of wonder and of dread. (Nm 20,12) In his judgments, no less than in man's obedience, is the Lord's glory revealed and his holiness unfolded; for his judgments as well as his commandments show his repugnance to evil and his determination to see the triumph of goodness. (Ez 28,22) Never has his holiness been more manifest, however, than in the One "who knew nothing of sin," who "went about doing good," and so loved the Church—and in her all mankind—that he had himself fastened to the wood of mercy in order to cleanse and lead her to glory. (2 Cor 5,21; Ac 10,38; Eph 5,25f) [3]

THE ONE GOD AND HIS MANY NAMES   "Hear, O Israel! The Lord is our God, the Lord alone!" is the Old Covenant's supreme proclamation; it is not forgotten in the New. One, unique, he must be loved and adored with an undivided heart. (Dt 6,4f; Mk 12,29; Mt 22,37) Israel's faith in the one and unique God was not the fruit merely of a special religious bent; it was a gift. Nor was it a development from primitive to advanced religious concepts. In his study, *The*

---

[3] On the Church's sanctification through the Lord Jesus, St. Thomas has this to say: "That the Church be glorious, having neither spot nor wrinkle (Eph 5,27), is the ultimate goal to which we are led by the Passion of Christ. This will come to pass when we have reached the Father's house, not while we are on the way to it. For were we to say 'that we have no sin, we [would] deceive ourselves.' (1 Jn 1,8)" (S.Th., 3ª,8,3, ad 2)

Old Testament Against Its Environment, the American scholar G. Ernest Wright makes an excellent case against the false application of the idea of evolution to the religion of Israel. The history of the ancient Hebrews was to a large extent a struggle between the supernatural vision given them and the natural outlook which was the preserve not only of primitive tribes but also of civilized nations. Among many examples of this strife are Laban's pursuit of his daughter Rachel who had stolen his household idols (Gn 31,19-24) and the pressing question the prophet Elia—disdainfully named "troubler in Israel"—put to his people: How long are you going to limp on both legs, how long to dance for Yahweh and for *baal?* (1 Kgs 18,21) The Old Testament is not the story of the advance of a people from polytheism to monotheism. The polytheist is too enmeshed in the web of nature's attractions and threats to break out of it. Abraham, the son of moon-worshippers, did not free himself but was freed by grace, by a divine summons.

Yahweh is Lord alone. Still, the Old Testament knows God by many names, several of which are, indeed, of pagan origin. They bear witness, not only to Israel's geographical proximity to her neighbors but, even more, to the already mentioned spiritual conflict. They are the fruit of an intense combat of which Israel's wars were the concomitants or sequels. A telling example is *baal,* "lord," the name the Chanaanites gave to their god. For a time, the ancient Hebrews themselves applied this title to the God of revelation, convinced that it was rightly his and his alone. Again, it is not impossible that the name Yahweh, though in slightly different forms, was used also by tribes and peoples other than Israel. Assuming this to be a fact for the sake of argument, does it prove that Israel's God is not unique and Israel's faith not singular? On the contrary. Rather than a mere imitation of pagan thought, Israel's response to him had conversive power. Whatever she touched, she changed. In borrowing from pagan awareness of things divine, she made the pagan gropings a vessel into which God could pour his revelatory message.

Though Israel stood apart as the bearer of God's message, she belonged to a large cultural community. It is no surprise, then, that she adopted a term that was the common possession of Semites. To most members of the Semitic language family, *el* designated the deity. The word may have derived from a root that means "to be strong," or from one that indicates "might" and "authority." If so, *el* would denote "head" or "chief." Still another theory seeks the origin of *el* in the preposition *'el,* "toward." In that case, *el* would be the one toward whom man turns for help and protection, to whom he directs his prayer and renders worship. Whatever its etymology, *El* became one of the Old Testament designations for the true God, as did *Elohim.* When used as a simple plural, *elohim* stands for gods, spirits, or angels, but when used as a plural of intensity, it bespeaks the concentration of all that is divine in one Being. As such, it served Israel well. In the happy view of the Belgian exegete Paul van Imschoot, *Elohim* enabled the chosen people to stress, against the multiplicity of circumscribed gods, the unity of him who is fullness, wealth without limit.

At times, *El* appears in combinations like *El-olam,* "the eternal God" (Gn 21,33), or more often, particularly in the patriarchal period, in the compound *El-shaddai.* A linguistically intriguing name, it has been variously translated as "God the Almighty," "the All-ruler," or "the towering, the most high God," or "God-the-mountain," that is, the constant and reliable One, the God who is a

14

sure refuge. The latter meaning would be akin to the frequent designation of the Lord as "Rock," "my Rock," "Israel's Rock." (Pss 17[18]32; 143[144]1; Gn 49,24) As the "Song of Moses" rejoices in him, the Rock whose deeds are perfect and whose ways just, so one of the psalms extols him as "our Shield" and another—at least in the original Hebrew—as Israel's "Habitation." (Dt 32,4; Pss 83[84]10; 89[90]1) The praise of God as Israel's Abode worked toward the invitation-to-come: Abide in me, as I do in you! Abide, dwell in my love. (Jn 15,4.10)

So numerous are the divine names that their listing and interpretation would fill page after page. Some are obvious: "my Lord," "our Lord," "the Lord of lords," "the God of heaven," "the God of heaven and earth." One, however, *Yahweh Tseba'ot,* "the Lord Sabaoth," holds a prominent place in the Church's liturgy; as part of the angelic "three times holy" (Is 6,3), it concludes the Preface, the hymn that sounds the "Thanksgiving" we call the Mass. *Tseba'ot,* "hosts," are either the heavenly armies or the powers of earth and heaven. In the first instance, *Yahweh Tseba'ot* might be rendered as "Yahweh, the angel-surrounded"; in the second, it would proclaim the One whom all things must serve as their origin and end. Again, God is called "the Awe of Isaac" and "the Mighty One of Jacob" (Gn 31,42; 49,24), he is hailed as "King" and as "Shepherd." (Pss 23[24]8; 22[23]1) Because of his untiring affection for the people he chose, the prophets portray him as a vinedresser planting a vineyard, a husband unwilling to abandon his unfaithful wife. (Is 5,1–7; Os 2,16ff) The tenderness of a mother is his, and so is a father's care and pity. (Is 49,15; 64,7; Os 11,1–4) For the ancient Hebrews, the divine names were more than appellations. God's name was his vicar; his presence dwelt in it, and thus his blessing, his strength. (1 Sm 25,25; Nm 6,27; Prv 18,10)

THE FATHERHOOD OF GOD   The Old Testament belief in a God who is everything to his own is the heritage of Christians as is dependence on the fatherhood of God. All who now call him "our Father in heaven" may do so because the ancient Israel first implored:

> O Lord, hold not back,
> for you are our father.
> (Is 63,15f)

Not that the people of Israel were alone in speaking of God as Father. In the most spiritual of Greek hymns, that of Cleanthes of the third century B.C., Zeus, the ruler of Olympus, is called father and asked:

> Thy children save from error's deadly sway;
> Turn thou the darkness from their souls away.[4]

What distinguishes Stoic belief from that of Israel is that to the Stoics sonship was the result of being born a man, while to the Jews it was a divine gift accompanying Israel's election. To the Stoics, sonship said little more than rationality, a rationality that gave man the opportunity of becoming

15

---

[4] James Adam, trans., in *The Greek Poets,* Moses Hadas, ed. (New York: Modern Library, 1953), p. 289.

one with the cosmic order. To the Jews, sonship was part of the Lord's gracious love for them: a favor that allowed them to enter into a personal relationship with him.

Under the New Covenant, the Old Testament invocation of God as Father has assumed a new dimension, depth, and intimacy. "Father" has become the divine name overshadowing all others. Whenever a Christian calls God his father, he does so in union with the eternal Son, as a brother or sister in Jesus the Christ. Gospel and epistles have kept for future generations the original ring of the name as it came from Jesus' lips: *"Abba, Father."* (Mk 14,36; Rom 8,15; Gal 4,6) [5] The preservation of the Aramaic word is not due to a strange preference for unfamiliar sounds. On the contrary, *Abba* permits any man shyly to enter into the familiarity of Jesus' colloquy with his Father. *Abba* takes him into the intimacy of Christ's inner life and, in so doing, gives him a glimpse of God's infinite being: the mystery of the triune God.

MAN IN CREATION

To many modern minds, man is no more than a chance-child of little-known parents, a prank of nature, or a ripple on the sea of life. Far from being revolutionary, notions of this kind revert to the dismal myths of Babylon. The people of the Mesopotamian basin—Israel's cultural ancestors and neighbors—saw man as the unintended result of an ugly and savage war among the gods, the unloved effect of a murderous rivalry between the monster goddess "Chaos" and her slayer. Despite Israel's geographical closeness, her spiritual elite never succumbed to this mythological spell. No doubt, the inspired writer of the first chapter of Genesis knew the Mesopotamian epic describing the origin of the cosmos and of man. His story of creation, too, speaks of chaos and of darkness but in it they do not contend with the Creator or rebel against him. Ever their Master, he commands, and darkness turns into light, chaos into order. No less does the biblical vision of man differ from the myths of old and of today. Its first perception at the beginning of Genesis is obvious enough: Man is a creature of God who made the heavens and the earth and all they contain.

CREATION AS PRELUDE However true, the affirmation that man is God's creature is incomplete. Contrary to the *prima facie* assumption, the making of the universe and thus of man is, biblically speaking, not God's supreme activity. Because his other works follow on the laying of the world's foundation, they may seem to us of lesser importance; their frame appears narrow, as confined as is the earth when compared to the unmeasured sweep of the cosmos. This naïve view, so tempting to a man steeped in science, is not in accord with the biblical message. For the latter, the story of creation is part of a greater story. In the in-

16

---

[5] To understand its ring in Aramaic, one would have to think of the endearment "Papa."

tention of the inspired writers, and thus doubtlessly in that of their Inspirer, the first chapters of Genesis are but the preface to the whole of Scripture: to the entire account of God's saving design. To put it differently, the deep and heavy rhythms that tell of God's calling into existence light, land, and sea; fish, bird, and beast; and in the end man, are but the prelude to his dealings with the people of his choice, old and new.

The common perspective tends to reverse the order, particularly today, when the grandiose evolution of the cosmos becomes more and more impressive. Viewed astronomically, the universal story of mankind looks like a small-scale repetition of the unfolding of countless galaxies. The history of salvation appears even more limited; it seems to concern only a minute section of the entire annals of humanity. This, however, is not the way Scripture sees recorded and unrecorded history. In biblical perspective, creation is a salvific event, the first in a series. It leads to the calls of Abraham, Moses, and David; and through them, to that of the people of Israel. Their election, in turn, leads to the birth of Jesus, and his birth to the still greater events of his death and entrance into glory. Finally, from the crib, the cross, the tomb, and the mount of ascension, the places where our redemption was wrought, history moves—in God's sight speedily, in ours slowly—toward the final manifestation of his reign at the end of ages.

The interpenetration of God's creative and salvific activities is particularly manifest in the psalms. Take Psalm 73[74], for instance. Pleading with God to remember his covenant, Israel appeals to him as her King from ancient days, the Doer of saving deeds on earth. The psalm then continues to speak of him as the One who divided the sea, released spring and brook, fashioned sun and moon, fixed summer and winter. Thus the salvation God wrought is twofold: At the beginning of time, he mastered the primordial chaos; at the end of Israel's torment in Egypt, he crushed the dragon, that is, Pharao, foe of God's salvific scheme. As he made the dry land rise from the primeval waters, so he turned the depths of the seas into a way for the redeemed. (Ps 73[74]12–20; Is 51,9f)

When God raised David his servant, the singer of another psalm proclaims, he built firm the throne of his anointed. Like the sun, like the moon, that faithful witness in the sky, it will stand forever; it will become—such is the divine promise—the seat of the King-Messia. (Ps 88[89]29f.37f) "The favors of the Lord I will sing forever," are the psalm's first words. ("Favors of the Lord" stands for the Hebrew *chasidei Yahweh,* that is, Yahweh's gracious deeds, the manifestations of his covenant love.) Yet shortly after, the singer can proceed:

> Yours are the heavens, and yours is the earth;
> the world and its fullness you have founded. . . .
> Yours is a mighty arm. . . .
> grace and fidelity go before you.
> (Ps 88[89]2.12.14.15)

Both, then, the fixing of the world's foundations and the preparing of the messianic reign, are seen by the psalmist as the manifestations of God's salvific will.

This total vision, binding together all of God's doings, guides especially the Second Isaia. In one breath, he calls God Redeemer and Maker of all. (Is 44,24) To the prophet, the wonder of creation (the restraining of the water so that dry land could appear) and the wonder of the Exodus (the restraining of the water

17

so that the redeemed could pass over) are parallels, arms of one great embrace. (Is 51,10) The same vision dominates another oracle of the prophet of consolation:

Fear not, for I have redeemed you;
I have called you by name: you are mine.
(Is 43,1)

Thus he proclaims in the name of the Lord. Before offering the people God's comfort, however, the prophet introduces him as the One who created Jacob, who formed Israel. (Is 43,1)

A CREATURE UNTO SALVATION   In asserting the salvific significance of God's creative work, "salvific" is given its widest possible meaning. "To save" means to pluck from danger, particularly from a fatal one; to set free and thus make well. Hence, salvation is delivery from chaos, bondage, tyranny, and sin; it is delivery from the "dragons" and all the other mythological beasts some biblical writers use as portraits of the forces that, from the beginning to the end of history, threaten the ultimate destiny of man, Israel, and the Church. (Gn 3,1; Dn 7,2–8; Ap 13,1–9) Through his work of rescue, a savior brings shelter, security, freedom, victory, peace—in a single word, life. The Savior of saviors bestows these blessings superabundantly. The life he offers is life in and with God. In the light of Scripture's total vision, then, our earlier statement, man is a creature, must be amended to an even more exalted one: man is a creature unto salvation, a creature unto glory. Not only does he come from God, he is open to him. Masterpiece of God the Transcendent, he is called to transcend his own nature. He is assigned a role granted no other being on earth: In freely accepted dependence on God, he is to seek his own sanctification by grace, the hallowing of the world, the hallowing of the name of the Lord.

To look upon creation as a prologue to what Calderón called the "great theatre of the world" and upon sacred history as its climax; to claim with Scripture that the drama of salvation is like a *première*, like the real performance, and that all the rest is but preparation for Israel's deliverance from the shackles of Egypt and mankind's deliverance from the shackles of sin and death [6]; to attribute to man, inhabitant of this cosmologically unimportant planet, not a peripheral but a central place—all this must seem intolerable arrogance to many non-Christians and agnostics alike. Yet, the biblical writers would be unruffled by such a charge. They spoke of cosmic origins, not to engage in philosophical speculation or to enrich scientific knowledge, but to

---

[6] Though the second exodus greatly differs from the first, the two are not opposites. Israel was freed not only from political but also from religious bondage, not only from slave labor but also from the infectious ways of her pagan rulers. On the other hand, the deliverance Christ wrought was not merely one from the fetters of sin; redemption's final fruit and fullest manifestation will be the new heaven and the new earth. (See the final section of the last chapter.)

bring into relief the spiritual preeminence of man, the spiritual singularity of Israel, and the spiritual primacy of the Church.

Still, the histories of mankind, of ancient Israel, and of Christendom prove that there is truth in the accusation of arrogance: Christians as much as Jews, and Jews as much as other men, have often misused their favored state. To find the corrective for this profanation of privilege, one need not go far. Singularity, as Scripture conceives it, is always singularity of service. The Old Testament leaves no doubt whatever that Israel was freed for no other reason than to worship the true God, that she was summoned to his service, a service to be rendered in fear and in joy.[7] In the New Testament, those believing in Christ are called servants of the true and living God. (1 Thes 1,9) Jesus having been in their midst as one who serves, they are bidden to serve one another in love. (Gal 5,13; Lk 22,27) No other title given him binds the two covenants as closely as does "Servant of Yahweh": the Man of pain whose sufferings wrought reconciliation, whose stripes were the healing of sinners. (Is 53,4ff)

High though their office was, the apostles wished to be no more than "servants of Christ and stewards of the mysteries of God." (1 Cor 4,1) Being a terror to wrongdoers and therefore a defense of the upright, civil authorities, too, are said to be "the ministers of God." (Rom 13,6) The United States' designation of its government as "administration," the name "ministers" given to members of cabinet in other countries, even the term "civil service" are, whether recognized or not, of Christian inspiration. In our day, however, the ideal of service has been robbed of its luster; an unreal concept of equality, born of the oppression of men by men, has driven it into disrepute. Still, man cannot be true to his calling, he cannot come to maturity, much less advance to friendship (Jn 15,15), unless he serve. The Hebrew word for "service" or "work" is *avodah,* the corresponding Greek term *leitourgía.* Man, then, is a liturgical being; he is called to the divine service, to the work of worship.

A CREATURE OF FLESH   Both service and salvation are part of Scripture's total vision. In this as in other respects, wholeness is the key to the biblical understanding of man. Seldom does Hebrew thought sharply distinguish between man's soul and his body, never does it dissect him. Though he is described as a clod of dust into whose nostrils God blew the breath of life, as a heap of earth that can think, speak, will, act, believe, love, and pray, Scripture does not, like Plato, look upon the body as the soul's tomb nor upon the senses as the mind's prison. (Plato, *Gorgias,* 493A; *Phaedrus,* 250C) The book of Wisdom, it is true, speaks of the corruptible body that burdens the soul and the earthen shelter that weighs down the mind. (Wis 9,15) On the whole, however, the Bible knows no cleavage between the

19

---

[7] Ex 7,16; Jos 24,14; Pss 2,11; 99[100]2.

two, no inevitable opposition, only a marvelous union that will find its lasting fulfillment in the resurrection of all flesh.[8]

"All flesh" means "all men." Interestingly enough, the Old Testament has no precise word for body. Instead, its writers like to speak of *basar*, "the flesh," and of *nefesh*, usually translated as "soul," though its meaning is far wider. *Nefesh* may stand for "life," "desire," "emotion," "passion," even for "living being," or for what we would call "person," "self." So indubitable is the union of "flesh" and "soul" to the ancient Hebrews that they attribute bodily functions to *nefesh* and psychic functions to *basar*. In fact, so much is man seen as an organic unit that every member, every organ of his body, the reins no less than the bowels, can be said to represent and express the life of the whole.

We can give but a few instances of the interchangeable use of flesh and soul. Once they enter the wide lands promised them by God, Moses tells his people, they will be able to eat the meat their *souls* desire. (Dt 12,20) Strange as it may sound to a modern ear, the *flesh* is said to long for the Lord. (Ps 62[63]2) Again, having encountered the Lord's presence in his prayer, the psalmist sings for all to hear:

> Therefore my heart is glad and my soul rejoices,
> my flesh, too, abides in confidence.
>
> (Ps 15[16]9)

That his flesh can dwell securely is of great moment to him, for in biblical thought flesh points to man's earthly condition and is thus a synonym for "weakness," while *ruach*, "spirit," stands for strength. Yet, for all its infirmity, "flesh" never means sin. Only when the flesh boasts of an imaginary power, only when it trusts in itself, does it become an occasion for sin and thus God's adversary and man's enemy. (Rom 8,7; Gal 5,16–24) In professing that the Word was made flesh, we must keep the biblical significance of flesh in mind. For what we proclaim by the Word's enfleshment is no more and no less than the assumption of the frailty of human nature by the everlasting and ever-potent Word of God.

As creature, man shares the fragility and finiteness of all things; his span is brief, and death is relentless in coming. Like a blossom he appears, and then withers; his coming and going are as swift as a fugitive's. (Jb 14,2) Again, his days are like grass, like the flower in the field; the moment the wind has passed over, the flower is forgotten even by the spot on which it stood. (Ps 102[103]15f) At first glance, then, the fates of man and beast seem identical. According to the most melancholy book of the Bible, one dies as does the other; both have the same breath of life, and there is no

20

---

[8] In St. Paul's writings, "body" stands at times for the whole man; see, for instance, Rom 6,6. On the redemption of man's sinful nature, on the new life implanted in his being, on the liberation and resurrection of the body, organ of Christ and shrine of the Spirit, see Rom 7,24; 8,11.23; 1 Cor 6,15.19f; Phil 3,21.

advantage in being a man; everything is futility. (Coh 3,19) [9] Dramatic exaggerations like "all things are vanity" (Coh 1,2) are very much part of Hebrew speech; to be understood correctly, however, they must be balanced by other biblical sayings. For the psalmist, there is comfort and hope even in man's weakness. Though the generation in the desert broke the covenant, forgot the wondrous deeds that saved them, even rebelled against God, he spared them again and again. Why did he spare them who had deserved punishment a thousandfold? Because in his mercy, the Lord God "remembered that they were flesh." (Ps 77[78]39)

On the surface, man and beast share a like fate. Both are said by the writer of Genesis to have been created the same day: a biblical statement that bespeaks their biological bond. Both perished indiscriminately in the flood. Both are subject to the same laws of nature and thus exposed to the elements which respect neither one nor the other. Still, man and beast are not alike. As Scripture recounts man's littleness, so does it his rank; its vision is never halved. Man is solemnly told to govern the beasts and solemnly warned never to mate with them. "Cursed be he who lies with any animal," reads the Law. (Dt 27,21) Above all, man is the object of God's special providence and has an immediacy to him other creatures lack. While, according to the biblical narrative, all owe their existence to a divine command, man was not created till God took counsel, either with himself or with the assembly of angels. (Gn 1,26) The decision to make man sprang from the depths of his heart. On the vivid canvas of Genesis, the earth and the sea produce beasts and fish, but to bring forth man God himself acts. He is the Weaver who weaves every man in his mother's womb, the Craftsman who knits together bones and sinews. (Ps 138[139]13; Jb 10,11)

MAN, THE IMAGE To a philosopher of the great Western traditions, the root of man's personal dignity is his rationality. Scripture's vision is different. Not that it contradicts philosophy, but man's rational nature is not its main concern. His honor is rather that he is "known," loved, by God. What gives him his biblical rank is not his intellectual endowment but God's "efforts" on his behalf. As he is known, so he must know, in the full sense of the word. For Scripture, knowledge is not so much a conceptual or analytical grasp as an understanding that comes from humble submission and loving obedience. To know someone is to be united with him. It was not shyness that made Mary tell the Archangel: "I do not know man." (Lk 1,34) What to us may sound like a timid expression was to her the ordinary Hebrew idiom for marital intimacy. Again, Peter's denial: "I do not know the man" (Mt 26,72) does not mean: "I have never heard of Jesus," rather: "I am not one of his friends." To know God, then, is to be admitted to his company. So much is life in his presence the goal to which man is

21

---

[9] A fuller treatment of death and the afterlife, so essential for the understanding of the Old Testament vision of man, is given in the last chapter.

called that a man has not entirely realized his humanity unless he "knows" God. So much is this knowledge and intimacy man's final destiny that knowing God, the hidden One, and Jesus, his Epiphany, is unending life. (Jn 17,3)

Scripture's most arresting proclamation on man's dignity and calling is that he was made in the image and likeness of God. (Gn 1,26f; 5,1; 9,6) However faint his resemblance may be, the eminence of this title becomes clear when one remembers that eternal Wisdom itself is named "the spotless mirror of the power of God, the image of his goodness." (Wis 7,26) Even more remarkable, Christ himself is called God's Image. (2 Cor 4,4; Col 1,15) What is it, then, that makes man the image of his Creator? There are Jewish and Christian theologians who point to his upright, unbent posture, to his royal stance, as does Ovid, the pagan:

> All other animals look downward; Man,
> Alone, erect, can raise his face toward Heaven.
> (Ovid, *Metamorphoses*, I, 84ff) [10]

Others advert to his mind and will. What God has to perfection, man is given in the bud: the ability to understand what is true, to fashion what is beautiful, to do what is good. All these interpretations, however, suffer from a weakness: They single out one part of man or another. True to its total vision, Scripture sees the whole of man as the divine likeness.

According to the Near Eastern mentality, a divine image is a double of the godhead, hence the Old Testament proscription of carved or other manmade images of the Lord. But there is an image God himself has made: man. Thus man is his legitimate representative, his ambassador, his "presence" on earth. As such, he has dominion over all other creatures; he is to rule the earth and even the space around the earth; he is to people the land with his children, and thus portray God's sovereignty and fatherhood. In the name, in the power of the Lord, he is to combat the forces of evil. Moreover, he is to impress on the world not only his own stamp but, above all, the seal of God's kingship. This is a task so high that, once a man has understood it, he will seek to be "graced" and guided by Jesus, the Man of men, beg to be shaped in the likeness of the firstborn Son, hope to be transformed into him who is the uncreated Image. (Rom 8,29; 2 Cor 3,18)

MAN IN HIS TOTALITY   Total man means first man and woman, husband and wife: Scripture could not be plainer. (Gn 1,27; 1 Cor 11,11) As the Ancient Dispensation moved toward its end, however, there appeared among the Jews monastic communities like that of Qumrân. Wishing to be penitents, its members pledged themselves to poverty and obedience. Common property, worship, and study were the mainstay of their life. Though some were married, others seem to have sought God's pleasure

---

[10] Rolfe Humphries, trans. (Bloomington: Indiana University Press, 1955), p. 5.

through lasting continence. In the Bible itself, there is only one man expressly called to celibacy, Jeremia. His solitary life—his renunciation of the unique blessing that wife and children were to an Israelite of old—was meant as a warning to the men of his day: Heedless of God and of tomorrow, they would meet sword and famine. (Jer 16,1–4) The New Dispensation has not altered the fact that the complete man is husband and wife, parent and child. Deliberate virginity, which is its glory, is a work of supererogation; an anticipation of, and a witness to, the glorious existence-to-come—one of those marvelous exceptions that do not break but strengthen a rule.

Sacrifice is not limited to the single life. Before Adam could rejoice in the presence of Eve, a deep sleep came over him. Sleep is the brother of death. No true companionship, then, is possible unless a man dies to himself. The vivid narrative of Eve's creation from Adam's rib troubles many, though it ought not. It is a deeply poetic statement of the perfect physical and metaphysical correspondence between man and woman. "Bone of my bone, and flesh of my flesh!" (Gn 2,23), Adam delights. His exclamation is not only the Hebrew way of expressing a superlative, it is also "the first song of bridal love." (Albert Gelin) Simple though the narrative seems, it proclaims a theological truth: The love of spouse for spouse, their intimate union—"the two become one flesh," one being as it were (Gn 2,24)—is God's exalted gift. It is the height of the wonders of creation. So great a thing is the love that unites man and woman—not for a moment but forever—that it mirrors God's love for his people and Christ's love for his Church. (Cf. Eph 5,31f.)

Total man also means all men. When the beginning of Genesis says *adam,* Adam is the first man and, at the same time, mankind. Later in Scripture, *adam* may refer to man the person or man the community, to any man, every man. Again, "Israel," the name God gave to Jacob, one of the fathers of the chosen people, has become the name of the nation itself. As the story of Adam casts light on the story of every man, so does the life of Jacob anticipate the lives of his children and children's children. To Scripture, the patriarch and his stock are one; begetter and begotten cannot be severed. So interwoven are their fates that they form one body—in a way, one person. H. Wheeler Robinson has called this seminal phenomenon the Hebrew concept of corporate personality. The ancestor not only contains the issue of his loins, his descendants speak, act through him. Thus generation is bound to generation; time is bridged; past, present, and future coexist.

When Joshua wished to remind his contemporaries of the Lord's great deeds at the time of the Exodus, he spoke to them of the wonders *they* had witnessed, though it had been *their forefathers* who had seen God's grace and faithfulness at work. (Jos 24,1–8) Again, St. Paul's prophetic vision of a *future generation* of Jews accepting Jesus as the Christ moves him to declare that *all Israel* will be saved, that the *whole of the people* will find salvation. (Rom 11,26) Thus, on the one hand, a single generation, even an individual Israelite, can represent all the children of Israel. On the other

23

hand, the whole community can also take the place of, or foreshadow, one of its members. When the singer of Psalm 33[34] rejoices: "I will bless the Lord," he speaks in his own name but also in the name of all his fellow-worshippers. So does the psalmist who professes: "The Lord is my shepherd." (Ps 22[23]1) Further, in the Servant Songs, the Suffering Servant is first the people of Israel and then the One-to-come, he who is Israel's sum and summit, the embodiment of what is best in Israel and of all she should have been.[11]

To sum up: One stands for all, and all are gathered up in one. The Hebrew idea of solidarity is obviously not confined to Scripture; it runs through the whole of Catholic theology. Original sin, the sharing of grace and merit, the sacrifice of the Mass, cannot be understood without the oneness of ancestor and offspring, head and body, member and member.

THE INDIVIDUAL AND THE COMMUNITY; ISRAEL AND THE NATIONS   Scripture's total vision embraces the individual and the community. It is true, the awareness of individuality was not equally strong at all times. It could not have been the same in the days of the desert as it was in later days; the latter permitted a freedom that would have been impossible under the exigencies of a nomadic life. Still, when the ten commandments were given to the people, they summoned not only the community but also each of its members to action. The movement from the community to the individual member is reversed in Psalms 129[130] and 130[131], for instance. Surely, there could be no more intimate expression of piety than the anguished cry for pardon in the first and the protestation of childlike trust in the second. Still, the two psalms rising from the depths of the worshipper's being end, one with the assurance that God will redeem the people (Ps 129[130]8), and the other with the appeal:

O Israel, hope in the Lord,
both now and forever.
(Ps 130[131]3)

Similar to the tension between the individual and the community is that between Israel and the nations, between Jews and gentiles. The Bible's first regard is for Israel set apart for God's purpose. Yet, through all the anxieties of prophets and sages for their own kinsmen shines God's care for every people, every man. There is no denying it, Scripture commands segregation, but one of spirits, not of skins. Its purpose was to guarantee the purity of faith, not of blood. To separate men for no other reason than the color of their bodies is a notion the biblical writers do not condemn explicitly because it is one far too absurd to have occurred to them.

No doubt, the relationship between Jews and gentiles was not always what it should have been. After Israel lost her political independence, the originally friendly relations deteriorated. These human failings notwithstanding, the segregation of Israel from her neighbors was divinely willed: Her separateness was

24

---

11 The four poems describing the destiny of the Servant of Yahweh are to be found in Is 42,1–4; 49,1–7; 50,4–11; 52,13–53,12.

for the good of all. Her inspired writers begin the history of salvation, not with the call of Abraham, the father of the Jewish people, but with the creation of Adam, the father of the human race. Abraham, in turn, is chosen so that blessing may come to all the families of the world. (Gn 12,3; 22,18) A spirited psalmist proclaims God as King of all the earth. (Ps 46[47]8) A jubilant people calls on all nations to praise him. (Ps 116[117]1) A hopeful prophet promises that peoples from everywhere will march up to the mountain of Yahweh to be taught his ways. (Is 2,2f) And an ill-tempered man of God has to be reminded that God's concern is for the wicked Ninivites, too, that it encompasses not only the men of that city but her cattle as well. (Jon 4,10f)

CHAPTER TWO

SIN, PARDON, REDEMPTION

The biblical message is not one of ease. There are few pages of Scripture that do not tell the frightening story of man's failure: Graced by God, he is able to "dis-grace" himself. Made unto salvation, he often chooses doom instead. He is no less than God's image but, oddly enough, one that can dim, darken, even distort itself—one that often refuses to shine. Man's character as the one divine likeness among earthly creatures cannot be for-

feited—it is a constituent of his nature—but he is at liberty to turn this likeness into a caricature. Endowed with freedom, he, who ought to be God's
representative, can change into God's adversary. Known, loved, and thus
called to know and love, man has the power to disrupt the fellowship with
God that ought to crown his existence. He may fall; indeed, he has fallen.
He is a sinner.

THE GRAVITY OF SIN

It seems easier to break away from what is good than to hold on to it,
easier to yield to things that drag man downward than to follow those that
draw him upward—a fact not only borne out by the content of Scripture but
also reflected in its language. Biblical Hebrew uses several expressions for
man's dereliction. There is, above all, the adjective *ra'*, "bad," which has all
the shades of its English counterpart: "harmful," "evil," "wicked." There is
a host of other words—verbs with their corresponding nouns—which, rendered into English, mean: "to miss the mark," "to transgress," "to deviate
from the right path," "to go astray," "to do wrong," "to become guilty," "to
be unfaithful," "to commit treachery," "to rebel." At times, wickedness, crime,
sin, guilt, or fault carry much the same meaning, though their juxtaposition
in a given verse tends to smite us with the gravity of sin. (Ex 34,7; Ps 31
[32]5) At other times, the combined use of guilt, offense, and rebellion implies degrees of wrongdoing. (Jer 33,8)

THE HORROR OF SIN   As a rule, the inspired writers do not dwell on the
distinctions that are the indispensable equipment of moral theologians. Unlike
the latter, the biblical authors do not painstakingly separate sins venial from sins
mortal, though the degrees of evil and its many masks are far from unknown to
them. *Every* sin is a horror in the sight of God—this is the relentlessness as well
as the simplicity of their teaching.

Thus Ezechiel recalls, in a single breath, both cultic and moral prohibi-
tions. With the same vehemence, he castigates the people for ignoring the hungry
and the naked, but also for raising their eyes to idols; for exacting usury from
the needy, but also for coming near a woman during her monthly period. (Ez
18,5-9) No doubt, some of the ritual ordinances went back to olden times, to
the days when Israel had not yet been set apart from the nations. To refrain
from the consumption of blood was one of these primitive interdicts; it was born
of the fear of mingling "soul," with "soul," the animal's nature with that of man.
Freed of its rudimentary character, the prohibition was given the seal of the living God. In his name, the breaking of it was declared a sin so grievous as to
deserve death. (Lv 17,10)

Another example of the absence of sharp distinctions is the case of the involuntary sinner. True, an unwilled offense was treated less severely than one
fully willed. The defiant scoffer—so the Law demanded—was to be cut off from
the community, while the one who had inadvertently transgressed a command-

ment could be cleansed by a ritual offering. (Nm 15,27–31; Lv 4,27f) Still, he was a sinner. Abimelech, king of Gerara, for instance, who had taken Sara into his household on the erroneous assumption that she was Abraham's sister, was threatened with punishment though he had acted "with a sincere heart and with clean hands." (Gn 20,5)

Whatever the reasons for the blurred boundary line between formal and material sins may have been, Israel's providential role was not to discuss the many subtleties of moral science but to shout to the world the one unbending fact: Sin is "ir-response," disobedience, insubordination. Not only has the man of sin grown weary of service, he spurns, despises his Master, refuses to answer him, makes himself deaf to his call. (Is 1,4; 43,22; Mal 1,6) The worst ever said about the men ungrateful for the favors showered on them is the word of God himself, calling them "those who hate me." (Ex 20,5) A wall has been raised, a chasm has been dug between the sinner and his Master. (Is 59,2) Thrown into the deep, raging waters of affliction, he knows himself to be cut off from the sight of his everlasting Keeper. (Pss 129[130]1; 30[31]23) So anguished is this separation that once the sinner turns penitent, he not only acknowledges his misdeed, its unbudging presence, but bursts out:

> Against you, you alone, have I sinned
> and done what is evil in your sight.
> (Ps 50[51]6)

For all its negativity, sin is an act of great consequence. Nothing could be more mistaken than to belittle it: It has eminence and grandeur—a perverted grandeur, a hollow eminence. To trifle with it, as our age so often does, shows a value blindness that can no longer distinguish evil from playfulness, the spectacle of hell from the antics in a nursery. Metaphysically speaking, sin is a privation, a deed that lacks proper ordering to the Source of all being and all goodness. Seen with the eyes of faith, however, it is a tremendous reality: the taking of a stance, the severing of a love bond, a break with God, an assault on his heart. Through it, person turns from Person. Unless the "turning away" becomes again a "turning to," the end is loss of intimacy with God, indeed, a disintegration of man's innermost life.

THE DIMENSIONS OF SIN   In a way, the psalmist's confession: "Against you, you *alone*, have I sinned" is hyperbole. Lovers never measure their words: Earlier, he had refused to be loved, now he wishes to return to love's embrace. Hence the radical accusation of being no one's enemy but God's. The overall message of the Old Testament, however, is that every sin is an act against God *and* man. Not that the offense whose unambiguous aim is revolt against the Lord was confused with the one directed against a neighbor. (1 Sm 2,25) Still, God is the Protector, the Guarantor of the rights of every man. He is, in particular, the Defender of the poor, the Guardian of orphans and widows, the Friend of the needy. As the prophets never cease to remind us, oppressors and exploiters blaspheme the Lord's name. (Is 1,23f; 10,1f; Jer 20,13; Am 5,7–15)

The unnatural vices of Sodom were not only known to the seducers

28

and the seduced, they were also outcries whose thunder was heard in heaven. The Sodomites were evildoers and sinners against the Lord. (Gn 19,13; 13,13) Joseph, prodded by Potiphar's wife to lie with her, had no doubt that, were he to yield, his deed would be more than a matter between him and the woman or between him and her husband, it would be a thing most wicked—a sin against God. (Gn 39,9) Again, there was David the king who had Uria, one of the heroes of his army, slain because he had used Uria's wife to satisfy his lust and needed to conceal his sin. For a while, he might have deluded himself that he had done merely what others had done before; he might even have been presumptuous enough to persuade himself that he had done well in taking what was "his" by "royal right." Whatever he thought, he was told by Nathan the prophet: "You have despised the word of the Lord!" (2 Sm 12,9)

No affirmation could be plainer, firmer, than God's word to Israel: "Whoever touches you touches the apple of my eye." (Za 2,12) From this, there is only a short step to the realization that whoever touches his fellow touches God. The injurer of a neighbor injures the One whose unseen presence is with every man. Obviously, the injury inflicted on God must not be taken literally. God cannot be wounded in himself, but sin bursts the bond that ties him to his creature. He cannot be stabbed as if he were flesh and blood: "Is it I whom they hurt [by their idol-worship], says the Lord; is it not rather themselves, to their own confusion?" (Jer 7,19) The inviolability of God notwithstanding, there seems almost no limit to the damage sin can do. The sinner harms not only himself but other men as well; he harms the people of God. It was this social dimension of every misdeed that the prophets sought to hammer into the hearts of their hearers: Every sin lowers the spiritual level of the community; every sin blocks the free flow of grace. Sin, then, is an attack on God's covenant, be it with the Israel of old or with the Israel renewed.

Being an onslaught on the covenant, every offense is an offense against our brothers in God. This is why a Catholic confesses his guilt not only in the privacy of his heart but in the confessional, in the sight, as it were, of the community of the faithful. Though the self-accusation is made in the lowest possible voice, though the confessor's lips are sealed, the penitent kneeling before God kneels also in the presence of his brethren on earth and in heaven. As the priest, in administering the sacrament of penance, represents God as well as God's people, so the contrite sinner mends not only the torn bond between himself and his heavenly Father, but also that between himself and his fellow members in the body of Christ.

THE UNIVERSALITY OF SIN   Nowhere in the Old Testament does the term "original sin" appear, nor is the doctrine of mankind's involvement in Adam's plunge expressly taught. Man was to scale the mountain of grace. Instead, he hunted for the sham power of independence, and fell. Chapter three of Genesis does not say in so many words that the first sin mysteriously encompasses all men, only that one generation after another is drawn into the fierce struggle between good and evil. It was some seven hundred years after the recording of the Genesis narrative that Ben Sirach, while contrasting the falsity of some women with the trueness of others, declared:

> In woman was sin's beginning,
> and because of her we all die.
> (Sir 25,23)

Still later, the apocryphal Ezra Apocalypse exclaims, in a verse that may have been touched up by a Christian editor: "What have you done, Adam! Though it was you who sinned, the evil was not yours alone. It was ours, too, who are your offspring." (4 Esd 7,118)

Although the oneness of mankind with Adam the *sinner* is not the explicit instruction of the Hebrew Scriptures, they are nonetheless open to its teaching; in fact, they suggest it. Twice within the story of the flood of waters drowning a multitude of sinners is the general corruption of mankind exposed. (Gn 6,5.12) Moreover, a string of testimonies by king, preacher, and sage laments the precarious state of every man. Neither righteous nor blameless, he is no more than a house of clay built on dust, more easily crushed than a moth. (Jb 4,17ff) Alas, none is there without sin. (1 Kgs 8,46; Coh 7,20) True, there are the great men and women of the Old Covenant—its "just"—yet even they were not free from what might be called a miscarriage of goodness. In reading the Old Testament, one cannot avoid the impression that the sacred writers intentionally point to the ample share of Israel's leaders in the weakness of all men. For only One is there who is flawless, the Holy One of Israel. When Scripture calls the outstanding figures of the Ancient Dispensation just or when they themselves, pleading before God, claim to be just, "just" always describes one who strives for, not one who has already attained, God's full pleasure by the unblemished compliance with his will.

Hence the repeated question which answers itself as it is asked:

> Who can say, "I have made my heart clean,
> I am cleansed of my sin"?
> (Prv 20,9)

> What is a man that he should be blameless,
> one born of woman that he should be righteous?
> (Jb 15,14)

In the great *Miserere,* these general questions become a personal striking of the breast:

> In guilt was I born,
> and in sin my mother conceived me.
> (Ps 50[51]7)

30

It is hardly necessary to stress that the psalmist does not refer to the coming together of his parents. To the ancient Hebrews, marital relations were not only without stain, they were sacred. Nor does the penitent imply that he was born out of wedlock. It is not his father or his mother he accuses, but himself. The birthplace and the abode of sin is the human heart, which Scripture calls evil, sluggish, tortuous, hardened, which it finds so debased that, to be saved, man must be given a heart new and pure.

> A clean heart create for me, O God,
> and a steadfast spirit renew within me.
> (Ps 50[51]12)

THE SOLIDARITY WOVEN BY SIN   Each sin is the work and responsibility of him who commits it. Others, nevertheless, are bound to be drawn into its radius. Though its immediate consequences generally affect but a few, at times a sin engenders outlooks, mentalities, comportments, acts in hundreds of thousands, even in an entire community—patterns of thought and deed that are, if not contrary to the divine will, at least devious and full of peril. There is a solidarity of evil as there is one of good. Thus the prophets, Israel's watchmen and warners, were her sternest accusers. Feeling the burden of her sin as theirs, they also interceded on her behalf. In this spirit, Jeremia begged the Lord:

> Remember that I stood before you
> to speak on their behalf,
> to turn away your wrath from them.
> (Jer 18,20)

More than a hundred years before, Amos had cried for pity and was heard:

> Forgive, O Lord God!
> How can Jacob stand?
> He is so small!
> (Am 7,2)

Ezechiel was even told to portray, in symbolic acts, the siege of Jerusalem and the exile of his people under Nabuchodonosor and, by his enactment, to "bear the sins of the house of Israel." (Ez 4,5)

Holy Scripture never speaks of sins in terms unrelated to life. Its narratives are concrete. Yet, the particular is at the same time the universal. The failings, little or great, of the people of Israel reflect those of Christendom, too. Looking at the biblical passages that tell the drama of Israel's many rebellions is like looking into mirrors, all unflattering to the spectator. They show him how marred his whole conduct really is—none more candidly than the account of Adam and Eve. The story of early man is, in a way, that of every man. The test and headlong dive into the pit of evil is not a solitary experience. The angel of darkness clothed as an angel of light, pretending to be man's friend and accusing God of being an enemy petty and envious of his creature's happiness; the distortion of the commandment so that it appears unbearable and its breaking almost a duty; the somewhat extended struggle and the rash decision; the distress and desolation following upon it; the excuses and shiftings of blame; the hiding, indeed, the flight from God who is now seen as Judge and Avenger,

31

no longer as the Forgiver—all this is a peerless piece of observation and introspection. By his delicate intimations, by some slight turning of phrases—all of it the feat of an accomplished artist—the inspired author succeeds in describing the very essence of our lapses.

The sacred writer, however, is more than a psychologist, he is a theologian. For him, Adam's sin—and by implication that of Adam's children—is a dread-full but vain attempt to make his will the measure of things, to become the only master of his deeds. Against the rules of logic, this fateful story of human solidarity—of the bond that, through the heritage of sin, ties all the sons of Adam to their ancestor—does not end in despair. It is also the story of God's solidarity with man, one announcing hope, indeed, victory; it is the beginning of the history of salvaticn.

The disaster in paradise has its counterpart in the desert. (Ex 32,1–6) There, Israel suddenly feels alone; no longer does she sense God's love, no longer does she value the covenant that had made her the Lord's very own. A prolonged absence of Moses, the mediator between herself and her divine Deliverer, tried her faith and found it wanting. The Invisible seemed withdrawn, the One who cannot be touched as if nonexistent. Thus the people demanded of Aaron an obvious god to lead them as Moses had, and he made them a molten bull to worship, sacrifice to, dance around, and revel about.[1] Here was a god who could not demand obedience, all he could do was obey his devotees. In the apt phrase of Father Stanislas Lyonnet, "instead of 'walking with God' [Israel] wanted God to walk with her." (*Vocabulaire de théologie biblique,* col. 777) Her rebellion (Dt 9,7) was lack of trust, fear to give herself wholly into the hands of the Lord.

So grievous did the rabbis of old judge the idolatry of their people that they saw in the suffering and bondage, the evil and unrest, the burdens and anxieties of later days, a punishment for the wrong of the desert generation. (Louis Ginzberg, *The Legends of the Jews* [Philadelphia: Jewish Publication Society, 1942], III, 120) Again, present and future seem so bound to the past in the solidarity of guilt that one could call the apostasy of the people in the wilderness Israel's "original sin," a parallel to the original sin of mankind. Once more, as in the garden of peace, so in the barren desert, human co-responsibility was matched, nay, surpassed by divine fidelity. Pity prevailed: God's anger dissolved into mercy, punishment into promise, and doom into hope. (Ex 32,11–14)

THE WONDER OF PARDON

So great is sin's terror that it seems to dominate the Old Testament. In reality, it is grace that is God's first and last word. The sinner may resist, hinder, retard, counteract the run of history, but only for a time. He cannot prevent the course of goodness from moving slowly but surely toward its prize. "The hand of the Lord is not too short to save." (Is 59,1)

---

[1] The worship of the golden calf is one of the many popular misreadings of Scripture. It is seen as the first sign of the prostration before the power of gold or money of which Jews are often accused. A careful reading of the text, however, shows the opposite to be true. In order to be able to dance around the sacred bull—the idol reminding them of their life among the Egyptians—Israel's women had to part with all their jewelry. (Ex 32,2f)

32

His thoughts are as high above ours as is heaven's canopy above the earth: Great and generous is his forgiveness, rich and abundant his pardon. (Is 55,7ff) These Old Testament assurances, comforting as they are, are topped by the inimitable solace of the New: "If our heart condemns us, God is greater than our heart and knows all things." (1 Jn 3,20)

THE OPEN DOOR OF CONVERSION   On a few occasions, the prophets seem to arrive at the end of their endurance. They can plead no more. Thus Jeremia throws these questions at the inhabitants of Jerusalem:

> Can the Ethiopian change his skin?
> the leopard his spots?
> And you, are you able to do good
> who are accustomed to doing evil?
> (Jer 13,23)

The city is so hardened by sin that it "cannot" change; it will be scattered like chaff by the winds of God—this, the prophet's denunciation, is no final judgment. As long as man breathes, as long as a community lives, there is always before them the miraculous possibility of conversion, of repentance. The Hebrew verb most often used for this renewal of one's existence is *shub*, "to turn away," "to turn to," "to return." Turning, then, is man's unique opportunity.

Various were the means by which the ancient Hebrews sought to regain God's favor. Though in the course of Israel's history these approaches were made deeper and purer, particularly under the loving scourge of the prophets, they all have this in common: Each is a spoken or unspoken acknowledgment of a wrong done and a conviction that God alone could set it right. True, the people were tempted, time and again, to use these rites as a sort of magic for the "placating of God's anger." But, shout the prophets, there are no unfailing "techniques" of reconciliation; God is ever—in his pardon no less than in his other works—the Sovereign whose gifts are uncompelled, gladsome, and free.

An ancient rite of expiation was "ransom": The life of Jonathan, Saul's son, for instance, was spared despite his breach of a cultic ordinance because the people "redeemed" him. (1 Sm 14,45) Perhaps another member of Israel's army took his place.[2] More profound than the act of ransom was the

---

2 To a Christian, this form of ransom seems hard, and there are even harsher instances than this one. (Cf. 2 Sm 21,6–9.) No matter how repellent these and, even more so, some nonbiblical attempts to rectify a wrong may have been, they were human gropings toward justice, gropings that found an altogether new and perfect, that is, loving fulfillment in Christ's ransom on the cross. Israel's history, particularly that of her beginnings, is filled with many instances of what to us is definite cruelty. The chosen people was still the captive of its environment, not having been able to shed the merciless laws of victory that were the common rules of the day. Where the unbeliever finds but darkness, the believer sees light: God, a humble and patient sculptor, let his people think for a while that these rules were his, only to lead them little

33

work of intercession whose luminous example is Moses' plea for pity. Anxious to atone for Israel's "grave sin" of having had a golden bull take the place of Yahweh, her unseen Deliverer, he begged the Lord not to let his anger blaze forth but rather to remember his sovereign pledge to Abraham, Isaac, and Jacob and thus forgive. Should God not be willing to pardon the people's desertion, Moses asked to be stricken from the book of the living. (Ex 32,1–14. 30ff; cf. Nm 17,11–15; Wis 18,21.) Did he wish to die *with* them or *for* them? Did he wish to "pay" for their apostasy or to end a mission that had failed? In any case, so urgent, so loyal was his entreaty that it became the model for St. Paul's prayer to be estranged from the Christ to whom he belonged with every fiber of his being so that his kinsmen might be close. (Rom 9,1ff)

Finally, there were expiatory offerings and sacrifices, prescribed by the Law, which reached their climax in the sacred customs of the Day of Atonement. (Lv 16) The slaughtering of the bullock and the shedding of his blood, the sending into the wilderness of a scapegoat laden with the people's sins—these and all the sacrificial rites of the Old Covenant show that man cannot cleanse himself but must be washed clean by another, that he cannot pardon his own wrongs but must appeal to the one and only Pardoner: God.

By cries and wailings, the penitents of Israel—individuals as well as the community—tried to give evidence of the earnestness of their pleas. Ascetic practices like self-laceration, the rending of garments, wearing sackcloth or tying ropes around the head served the same purpose. (Os 7,14; 2 Kgs 19,1; 1 Kgs 20,31f)

> Gird yourselves and weep, O priests!
> Wail, O ministers of the altar!
> Come, spend the night in sackcloth,
> O ministers of my God!
> (Jl 1,13)

was a typical call to the Lord's servants to mourn and lament with the whole assembly of the faithful that the "withered joy" (Jl 1,12) might green again. Similarly, the lamentations of Jeremia pierced the skies:

> The joy of our hearts has ceased,
> our dance has turned into mourning:
> The garlands have fallen from our heads:
> woe to us, for we have sinned!
> Over this our hearts are sick,
> at this our eyes grow dim. . . .
> Lead us back to you, O Lord, that we may be restored.
> (Lam 5,15ff.21)

---

34 by little to greater moral refinement. Suppose an uncultured spectator had been looking at the rough block that had just come under Michelangelo's hammer and chisel—the block from which his mighty Moses was to appear. The onlooker might have cried out: "How crude! This will never amount to anything!" But Michelangelo's day-by-day work was able to bend the marble and transfigure the cold stone into a figure on fire so that now the lightning of Sinai can be seen and its thunder heard.

THE PENITENTIAL LITURGIES   Corporate confession, the public admission of sins by all, was one of the glories of ancient Israel. For it is supernatural to unveil, nay, to tear off the screen all men like to spread over their failings. In the book of Daniel, we have one of the latest and most stirring examples of a prophet as the penitential spokesman of his brethren:

> Ah, Lord, great and awesome God,
>   you who keep your merciful covenant
>   toward those who love you and observe your commandments!
> We have sinned, been wicked and done evil:
> We have rebelled and departed from your
>   commandments and your laws. . . .
> Justice, O Lord, is on your side;
> We are shamefaced even to this day. . . .
> But yours, O Lord, our God, are compassion and forgiveness!
> (Dn 9,4–9)

To say it again, the prayers of atonement, the cries of supplication, the penitential songs,[3] are part of Israel's splendor. For never is a man so high as when he bends low before God.

Happily, Scripture has preserved, not only for our study but for our use, samples of Israel's penitential liturgies. Here is one:

> Even though our crimes bear witness against us,
>   take action, O Lord, for the honor of your name—
> Even though our rebellions are many,
>   though we have sinned against you.
> O Hope of Israel, O Lord,
>   our savior in time of need! . . .
> You are in our midst, O Lord,
>   your name we bear:
>   do not forsake us!
> (Jer14,7ff)

Here is another example, even more powerful:

> We have all withered like leaves,
>   and our guilt carries us away like the wind. . . .
> Yet, O Lord, you are our father;
>   we are the clay and you the potter:
>   we are all the work of your hands.
> Be not so very angry, Lord,
>   keep not our guilt forever in mind;
>   look upon us, who are all your people.
> (Is 64,5–8)

The most remarkable thing about these confessions is that their hope is not based on the people's shame, rue, promise of reform, not on their inner suffer-   *35*

---

[3] Among the supplicatory psalms are Pss 59[60], 66[67], 78[79], and 82[83]. The penitential psalms the Church has appended to the breviary are Pss 6, 31[32], 37[38], 50[51], 101[102], 129[130], and 142[143].

ings or outer efforts; it is based on God's doing: on what he can and—so the penitents unswervingly trust—will do. They rest their destiny on his grace. Who would contest, then, that not only the faithful in Israel but also her sinners, penitents, and pardoned are the spiritual ancestors of Christians?

In its pleas for forgiveness, the Old Testament anticipated one of the doctrines which is at the heart of Catholic theology: the interplay of the divine and the human in the act of justification, that is, the concurrence of Creator and creature, of God the All-holy and man the undeserving sinner. God's sovereignty, holiness, and grace do not annul man's freedom. On the contrary, they do—and they alone can—bring it to its full realization. Justification of the sinner is not partly the exhausting march of the returning prodigal and partly the happy pace of the outrushing father; it is wholly God's work and wholly man's. On the one hand, Zacharia urges his people: "Return to me, says the Lord of hosts, and I will return to you!" (Za 1,3) On the other, Jeremia puts this petition into the hearts of the wayward: "Make me return, and I shall return." (Jer 31,18) Again, in the mighty psalm of imploration, a triple cry mounts to the Shepherd of Israel that he be gracious: *Elohim hashibenu,* "Restore us, O God!" shouts his flock. He alone, the Lord of hosts, is the community's hope. If only he let his face be bright again, salvation would be theirs. (Ps 79[80]4.8.20) Still, in Yahweh's name, the prophets do not cease begging the people to be in earnest about their conversion; to turn, each one of them, from his evil course; to reform, each one, his ways and doings. (Jer 18,11)

THE DELIGHT OF THE FORGIVER   In one of her prayers, the Church calls God "Restorer and Lover of innocence." (Wednesday after the Second Sunday of Lent) The sequence in this invocation seems like a slip of the tongue, but it is not. That there should be greater joy in heaven over an earnest penitent than over ninety-nine self-acclaimed just is only right. Yet, that those who lost their innocence and had to regain it should outrank those who persevered and never strayed off the road of fidelity, indeed, that they should be closer to God's heart seems unbelievable. The truth is that, without distinction, all of us have sinned, have lost God's glory and cry, whether we know it or not, for the favor of his redeeming grace. (Rom 3,23) The title "Restorer and Lover of innocence," with which the liturgy hails God, joyfully spells out the paradox of pardon.

The inspired writers of the Old Testament are not quite so bold, but they do praise God as the Maker and Mender of men. They speak of him as the One who delights in his promise of fidelity, his oath of grace, in his clemency and compassion. (Mi 7,18ff)

> It is I, I, who wipe out,
>   for my own sake, your offenses;
>   your sins I remember no more. . . .

36

> I have brushed away your offenses like a cloud,
>   your sins like a mist;
>   return to me, for I have redeemed you.
>   (Is 43,25; 44,22)

The thoroughness of divine absolution is reflected in the expressions Scripture uses. According to Michea, Israel's sin is not only pardoned, her guilt not only removed—God treads them under his foot, he even hurls them into the deep of the sea. (Mi 7,18f) No one phrase is rich enough to tell the wonder of forgiveness. "To take away," "to blot out," "to efface," "to dismiss," "to deliver," "to heal"—these and other verbs are only approximations of what happens between the divine Pardoner and the human sinner. The Lord's design is not merely the destruction of this or that sin but the giving of a new spirit that will transform sinner into saint, foe into friend. (Jer 31; Ez 36)

Still, is forgiveness really possible? Something done, after all, can never be undone. True enough, but an evil deed exists in two realms, as it were: that of fact and that of meaning. If a man curses or kills, the words or deeds "remain." Their factualness notwithstanding, man's sorrow and forgiveness can, through the power the grace of God bestows on them, change their significance and direction; they can even make evil work unto good. Granted this possibility, some may argue, is pardon not an anomaly, an aberration, a breach of all norms of justice, indeed, the antithesis of God's inviolable integrity? So it would seem to our limited horizon, but not to his infinite being:

> My heart is overwhelmed,
>   my pity is stirred.
> I will not give vent to my blazing anger.
> No longer will I destroy Ephraim.

(Os11,8f)

His pity is not acquired, nor his mercy borrowed. They are his nature. It is for his own sake, he declares through the Second Isaia, that he will make an end to sin. (Is 43,25) Again, he affirms that the death of the wicked man pleases him not, rather is it his holy lust to see him live. (Ez 18,23) To see him *live*—not merely subsist, not merely vegetate but enjoy the abundant life that is reserved for those who dwell in, with, and for God.

THE ABUNDANCE OF REDEMPTION

Sin is a hanger-on, worse, a parasite draining man of his last drop of blood. To remain within the imagery of Scripture, the sinner is like one sunk in a fetid swamp, where there is no foothold, where the water closes in on him, ruthlessly mounting to his throat. Yet, even in his wretchedness there is hope: God's saving help, grace, and love. With the Lord there is abundance of redemption. (Pss 68[69]2f.30; 129[130]1.7) Indeed, redemption is Scripture's paramount theme. Forgiveness, pardon, and ransom are like melodies in a great fugue, repeated again and again till they reach their climax in the breathtaking *Exsultet* of the Easter Vigil.

O truly necessary sin of Adam blotted out by the death of Christ,
O happy fault to merit a Redeemer so pure, so strong.

Adam's sin was "necessary" because it made possible the disclosure of what would otherwise have remained hidden: the extent of God's "involvement" with man. With his bleeding hand, Christ cancelled our debt; with his crucified body, he crossed out our misdeeds; with a love never seen before, he turned the load of guilt into a lever of grace. The morning put darkness to flight.

It is Judaism's contention that the world is unredeemed, unchanged. No one would be so foolish as to deny that sin, suffering, tears, and death are still with us. The redemption wrought on the cross is one offered to, not imposed on, the sinner. Abundance is there for the asking but it must be asked for with might and meekness. Redemption cannot burst into its flaming blossoms—as nature does in spring when it turns the ground into a carpet of beauty and the trees into a roof of joy—if Jesus, "Prince and Savior" (Ac 5,31), is not accepted by all, Israel included. Yet, even now guilt can be ended, tears stilled, suffering muted, death overcome. St. Paul proclaims in what could be called a little summary of the Christian message that no matter how much sin abounded, grace abounded the more. (Rom 5,20) Though man's entanglement is wide and deep, God's mercy is wider and deeper still.

THE VOCABULARY OF REDEMPTION   Two Hebrew words, above all others, show the ascending movement throughout Israel's history from "redemption" to redemption, from partial to total deliverance. The first is *padah,* "to pay ransom," the other *ga'al,* "to vindicate." Originally legal terms, both leave the rough realm of rights and duties behind for one greater and more benign.

Ransom.   The Mosaic law determined, among other things, that should an ox, through the culpable negligence of its owner, gore a man or woman to death, the ox would have to be stoned. Its master, too, would have to die. But the Law permitted him to escape the death penalty by imposing a fine upon him; through the payment of a ransom, *pidyon,* whose amount was probably stipulated by the bereft family or by judges, the doomed man could save, or "buy back" his life. (Ex 21,28ff) Again, if a man purchased a girl, wishing to adopt her into his household and later to make her a wife second to his first, but as time passed found her no longer attractive, he could not sell her to a strange family "because he has broken faith with her." Two ways were open to him: He could give her to his son so that by becoming his daughter-in-law her dignity would be safeguarded, or he could offer her father the opportunity of ransoming her, that is, of buying back her freedom. (Ex 21,8f)

These two cases regarding personal injury of one kind or another are clearly matters of jurisprudence. Quite different is the ransom of every firstborn, be he the oldest son of a woman or the firstling of an animal. When Pharao stubbornly refused to see God's finger at work and disobeyed the command to let Israel depart, God forced Israel's release, Scripture relates, by slaying all of

38

Egypt's firstborn, men as well as beasts. Only the children of the Hebrews and the offspring of their animals were spared this bitter fate. (Ex 11,4–8; 12,29f) In memory of their preservation, the people were bidden by the Law to ransom every firstborn male child; to sacrifice the firstlings of all ritually clean animals, and to kill those of unclean beasts, unless a lamb were offered in their stead. (Ex 13,1–16; 34,19f)

The consecration of all firstlings to the Lord—their being set apart as the possession of God the Maker, and not of man the steward—is, no doubt, of greater antiquity than the biblical reference would indicate. But the biblical injunction, connecting the ancient rite to God's redemptive work, gave it a deeper meaning. Through the sacrifice and ransom of the firstborn, representatives of their kin, the Israelites were to be reminded of the Lord's strong hand that brought them out of Egypt, and thus they, indeed all creatures, were to be bound more strongly to him. So significant was the bond between him and the firstborn in Israel that their particular dedication to him leads the author of Hebrews to call the company of the redeemed, "the festive assembly and the Church of the firstborn who are enrolled in the heavens." (Heb 12,23) "You have been bought at a great price!" St. Paul tells the Corinthians. (1 Cor 6,20) The price was infinite. For there is no conceivable equation between man's debt and Christ's blood—the stream of love that brought release to the debtor.

Analogously, the sum of five silver shekels which the Law fixed for the redemption of every firstborn in Israel (Nm 18,16) was never meant to be a "fair" amount. The relationship between God and man is above mere fairness. Five shekels—in modern currency about nine dollars—were for the many poor in Israel a considerable amount. Still, they were only a token. Even if someone had offered a mountain of silver, it would have been no more than a mite of gratitude and submission to the Lord of life, to Israel's Deliverer. He had freed the Hebrews from the decomposing forces of Egypt that had torn apart their individual as well as their communal existence and had thus given them the opportunity of centering their lives in him.

That ransom money had to be paid for the firstborn, and is still being paid by observant Jews, seems to intimate that man's natural state is far from sufficient. In any case, the incommensurability of a few silver coins and a human life shows that man's offering does not render measure for measure but something measurable for something immeasurable. The great principle of equity is set aside in favor of grace. Though not redemption in its ultimate sense, the redemption of the firstborn is possible only because God is gracious or—as the Jewish liturgy, echoing Scripture, declares—because the Lord is our Blesser, Keeper, and Guardian, because he is Shade, Peace, and Presence. (Nm 6,24ff; Ps 120[121]5–8)

Vindication.   The same cleansing, ennobling process that marks the use of *padah*, "to ransom," marks that of *ga'al*, "to vindicate." With a steadfast hand, crudity and coarseness are removed to make it a fit description of God's own work. One of the most ancient and widespread customs of human society is that of blood vengeance: bloodshed demanding bloodshed. Its origin lies partly in man's lower passions, partly in a mistaken sense of honor and solidarity. For a primitive society, devoid of a ripened legal system and due process of law, the principle of atoning the blood of a murdered man by the blood of his murderer was almost a necessity for upholding a minimum of justice. More than that, it acted as a dam against hatred of brother for brother, against the defilement of the land in the midst of which the Lord himself willed to dwell. (Nm 35,33f) As a measure of elemental justice, blood vengeance found its way into Scripture:

> Whoever sheds the blood of man,
> by man shall his blood be shed.
> (Gn 9,6)

Its publicly acknowledged agent was the nearest relative: Not only was it his right, it was his duty to avenge the loss of life and to restore the respect as well as strength of the injured family. "The avenger of blood, the *go'el ha-dam*, may execute the murderer, putting him to death on sight." (Nm 35,19)

No doubt, a young society, just having escaped nomadic life could not assume probity by the intricate system of law enforcement available to a civilized world. Thus blood revenge was tolerated by God for quite some time. We do not know at what period courts were able to take over the task of punishing a murderer. The Bible records what must have been early modifications of the stern rule of retribution. It refers to the hot anger of the pursuing avenger. (Dt 19,6) Aware of man's brutal inclinations, of his hostility so difficult to quell once aroused, the Law provided cities of refuge for those guilty of manslaughter. Most likely, the avenger would make no distinction between one who had killed with deliberation or malice and another who had done so unintentionally; the Law, however, gave the inadvertent homicide the benefit of asylum and thus the chance of living securely. (Jos 20; Dt 19,1–13; Nm 35,9–29) It also granted the involuntary killer rest and safety at God's altar. (1 Kgs 1,51)

Another attempt to ease the adamantine rule of vengeance was the so-called *lex talionis*, the law of retaliation. At first hearing, it sounds like the most rigid enforcement of the rule of vengeance: "Life for life, eye for eye, tooth for tooth, hand for hand, foot for foot, burn for burn, wound for wound, stripe for stripe." (Ex 21,23ff) This law of tit for tat, of the inflexible correspondence between crime and punishment, has often been regarded as the quintessence of Old Testament morality. It is not. Incidentally, the law of retaliation did not originate with the ancient Hebrews—it has its parallels in the Code of Hammurabi and is part of the general Semitic background that shaped so much of early Hebrew life. Quite apart from its non-Hebrew origin, in its biblical context it must not be read: "Take at least an eye for an eye!" rather: "Take an eye for an eye— and no more!" It must not be understood as if it were to enjoin: "Take eye for eye, and relish the taking!" rather: "Take eye for eye, and let there be an end to strife."

Strange though it may sound, the biblical law of talion was one of moderation. It sought to bridle man's instinct; to curb, rather than encourage his lust for reprisal; to establish unassailable ratios—standards, that is, not subject to caprice. Stranger still, the maxim of retaliation was to make Israel understand ever more deeply God's proclamation that *his* was the vengeance, *his* the retribution. (Dt 32,35; Rom 12,19) In the end, however, the principle of measure for measure, the delight of every legal mind, was found wanting. The demand that offense and penalty be exactly proportioned must needs deaden the mind's suppleness and the heart's warmth. Hence Christ's counsel that the measured course of justice be overridden by the unmeasured way of generosity. (Mt 5,38–42)

THE THEOLOGY OF REDEMPTION   It is the enduring marvel of Scripture that the language of ancient Israel became the means by which God's ways with man were revealed. The same vocabulary that served to describe man's redemption of a firstborn child or slave was used to extol God's redemption of the oppressed and the sinner. Though God obviously made no payment to Egypt's king for the release of the chosen people, he is said to have "ransomed [them] from the hand of Pharao." (Dt 7,8) His "ransom money" is the "fancy" he took to this downtrodden people, the inexplicable love with which he pressed it to his heart and, regardless of merit, made it his firstborn. In the book of Deuteronomy, therefore, Moses is able to rest his plea that God forgive Israel's rebellion on no other ground than that, in his majesty, he had "purchased" and brought her out of Egypt. (Dt 9,26) Israel in turn is bidden to be compassionate in her dealings with slaves because she was a servant once herself and owes her freedom only to God, her Ransomer. (Dt 15,15)

Not only for the community but for its individual members as well did the Lord "win" freedom. Isaia, for instance, calls Abraham the "ransomed," the redeemed, the first one to be taken out of the pagan enclosure in order to taste the freedom that crowns perfect faith. (Is 29,22) Again, David sees his delivery from every distress as a ransom wrought by God. (2 Sm 4,9) Some of Israel's men of prayer beg God to "ransom" them from their foes so that freedom and peace be theirs; to redeem them from the company of sinners that they may walk in integrity. (Pss 54[55]19; 25[26]11) With confidence, one of them proclaims:

> Into your hands I commend my spirit;
> you will redeem me, O Lord, O faithful God.
> (Ps 30[31]6; cf. Lk 23,46.)

Another psalmist declares that no man can pay ransom to God so as to remain alive forever. "Too high is the price to redeem one's life." Though none can avoid the grave, the "pit" cannot be God's last word, the singer knows. God will redeem him from the clutches of the netherworld. His trust that the Lord will receive him is like the first shimmer of a hope to which Christ's gospel gave the ultimate expression. Though the manner and mark of everlasting life are still unknown to the psalmist, there rises from his heart the gleam of a world in which the ruler is not death—the shepherd herding all into the bleak abandonment of Sheol—rather of a world in which death is swallowed up and victory won. (Ps 48[49]8f.15f; 1 Cor 15,55)

As *padah*, "to ransom," was harnessed to convey God's intervention on behalf of his people, so was *ga'al*, "to vindicate." Indeed, no harness was necessary. *Ga'al* and its corresponding noun *go'el* lent themselves most easily to their theological application. There were the days when Israel's tears mingled with the waters of Babylon, when bitter captivity shut her lips to the glad songs of the Lord. (Ps 136[137]1.4) Shortly before her liberation, it

41

seems, God awakened a prophet who, though firm like Isaia, proclaimed words of supreme consolation:

> Comfort, give comfort to my people,
>   says your God. . . .
> Her time of servitude is ended;
>   her guilt paid in full.
>
> (Is 40,1f)

With a tenderness unusual in those intrepid pursuers of Israel, he said:

> Fear not, O worm Jacob,
>   O maggot Israel;
> I will help you, says the Lord;
>   your redeemer is the Holy One of Israel.
>
> (Is 41,14)

Here and in a dozen other passages of the Second Isaia, "redeemer" stands for *go'el*, the relative who was blood-bound to vindicate his own. God's ties to Israel were, of course, those of love, of a wedlock entered into in perfect freedom; as such, they were stronger than those of blood. Still, he is said to have avenged his people, pursued her enemies like a warrior. A hero in her defense, he delivered her from the yoke of domination by idolators. Babylon the queen would now be in chains, and chained Israel a queen again:

> Shake off the dust,
>   ascend to [your] throne, Jerusalem;
> Loose the bonds from your neck,
>   O captive daughter Sion!
>
> (Is 52,2)

There can be no mistake, Israel's fetters were the consequences of her sin. Her prison garb was the mark of her defections, the garments of beauty she was now to put on were the sign of divine forgiveness. (Is 52,1)

> You burdened me with your sins,
>   and wearied me with your crimes.
> It is I, I, who wipe out,
>   for my own sake your offenses;
>   your sins I remember no more.
>
> (Is 43,24f)

The last verse has been quoted before, but it can hardly be repeated often enough since it shows the gratuity of Israel's delivery which—this, too, cannot be sufficiently emphasized—was one from political *and* spiritual serfdom. It is true, in the psalms the prayer as well as the rendering of thanks for the divine delivery seem—to the unbiblical ear—concerned merely with outward misery. To biblical man, however, the outer and the inner were intimately related. "Redeem me, have pity on me," the Israelite wor-

42

shipper cried out. He asserted his integrity in keeping the Law and shunning the company of the wicked yet, while doing so, he could not help but remember his struggle with evil and his past failings. (Pss 24[25]; 25[26]) Or, when in an hour of military defeat Israel implored God not to cast her off but to redeem her for the sake of his unfailing love, her first thought was, no doubt, delivery from her foes. But she was not unaware of the shadow of former rebellions. (Ps 43[44]) Indeed, it was more than a shadow that followed Israel. "My sins so overcome me that I cannot see," one psalmist confessed, and another: "Our hidden sins [you keep] in the light of your scrutiny." (Pss 39[40]13; 89[90]8)

No matter how often Israel's devout ask for delivery from bondage and pain, ultimate redemption is freedom *from* sin and *for* God. For Israel's Maker and Ruler, her Deliverer and Redeemer is truly her *Go'el,* her Next-of-kin. Through the grace of the covenant, Abraham's offspring have become his children:

> You, Lord, are our father,
> "Our Redeemer" is your name from of old.
> (Is 63,16)

He claims exiled Israel as his wife. Sing she must, be jubilant, and forget the shame of her loneliness: Her Creator has become her Husband, the God of all the earth her freedom-bringing Kin. (Is 54,1.4f) Nothing could proclaim more vividly that during the Ancient Dispensation God's redemptive acts tended toward the strengthening, the restoration, the renewal, and finally the broadening of the covenant. His deeds were for the sake of union, their purpose was at-one-ment.

> For a brief moment I abandoned you,
>   but with great tenderness I will take you back.
> In an outburst of wrath, for a moment
>   I hid my face from you;
> But with enduring love I take pity on you,
>   says the Lord, your redeemer.
> (Is 54,7f)

JESUS, ISRAEL'S AND THE NATIONS' GO'EL   With the coming of Jesus, the assurance: "With enduring love I take pity on you, says the Lord, your redeemer," is no longer addressed to Jews alone but to all who wish to be Abraham's offspring by faith. Again, one of Israel's singers, offering his good wishes to a newly crowned king, is carried away by the spirit and proclaims the coming of a ruler unlike any other:

> He shall rescue the poor man when he cries out,
>   and the afflicted when he has no one to help him.
> He shall have pity for the lowly and the poor;
>   the lives of the poor he shall save.
> (Ps 71[72]12f)

43

In Jesus, these words and other prophetic visions are fulfilled in a way that exceeded every expectation. At the synagogue of Nazareth, for instance, he presented himself to the people as the Bringer of glad tidings, the Healer of the brokenhearted, the Freer of captives, the Broadcaster of God's favor foretold by the prophet. But in doing so, he left out the final phrase of the Isaian passage announcing "a day of vindication." (Is 61,1f; Lk 4,18f) Was this omission deliberate so as to indicate that, in and with him, something new had entered history? Even though the New Testament does not expressly give him the title *Go'el*—or, rather, its Greek equivalent—the whole of it testifies that he is the Next-of-kin: Did he not call men his *brothers* and lay down his life for his *friends?* (Heb 2,11; Jn 15,13) "One God there is, and one Mediator between God and men, the *Man* Christ Jesus who gave himself as ransom for all," St. Paul proclaims (1 Tm 2,5f), while St. John delights in "Jesus Christ the Just," "our *Intercessor*," the Pleader of our cause before the Father, "the Atonement for our sins—yet not only for ours but also for those of the whole world." (1 Jn 2,1f)

What a Kinsman! He carries mankind's burden; he saves, not souls or bodies, but souls *and* bodies: the whole man. There is no greater realization of the wonder of the Ancient Dispensation, which revealed God as Israel's *Go'el*, than God's coming in the flesh. Made man, he is by this very fact man's Advocate, Ransomer, and Redeemer. All ailment and anguish he carries as if they were his own. In the purest sense, he is Israel's, he is everyone's blood brother. He *does* avenge murder and lust, injustice and contempt, hatred and envy, and all the other transgressions of man, but not by shedding the sinner's blood, rather by giving his own, surrendering his life "as a ransom for many." (Mt 20,28) He is the unexampled Avenger who vicariously "died for us," "died for our sins," "died for all." (Rom 5,9; 1 Cor 15,3; 2 Cor 5,14f)

When his heart was pierced, sin was speared. Not only was this sin and that one pardoned, sin itself received the deathblow. This is not to say that it has disappeared from the midst of men. At times, sin seems to be more virulent today than it was before the advent of Christ. This may or may not be so. On the one hand, it must never be forgotten how much Christ's word and work have sharpened man's conscience; on the other, the mightier God's offer of love, the mightier is man's temptation to reject it—such is his contrariness. Even if it could be proven that in the Christian era there have been sinners more inclined to wickedness than ever before, sin as a principle is dead. Sin is the will to do away with God, to "ungod" him. A Messia who is God-in-the-flesh, slain by the hands of men and risen from the dead, unmasks sin's futility. Though it battles still, it has lost the war.

44   In Jesus the Christ, we are set free, we are redeemed at the cost of his blood; our sins are forgiven because of the lavishness of his grace. (Eph 1,7) He is the Lion of Juda become the Lamb enthroned; the marks of slaughter are on him, the marks that proclaim the purchase for God, paid

in blood, of men of every tribe, tongue, people, and nation. (Ap 5,5–10) Purchaser and purchase are perfect but not so the purchased, even though they have been told: "Christ suffered for you, leaving you an example; it is for you to walk in his steps." (1 Pt 2,21)

The victory Christ won for the redeemed will not be wholly theirs, nor can they hold redemption's abundance without fear of loss till the day on which the fullness of God's glory will be manifest; but theirs is a mighty pledge. (Eph 1,14) Though the time between Christ's first coming and his second is still one of waiting and travail, of expectation and labor, the grace of the present is a foretaste of the freedom and splendor that will be their sure possession. (Rom 8,18–25) As the people Christ cleansed, marked as his own, and thus made eager to pursue what is good in his eyes (Ti 2,13f), they can say: "In hope were we saved." (Rom 8,24)

CHAPTER THREE

COVENANT, GRACE, PEOPLE OF GOD

Ancient Israel was a covenanted people, and so is the Church: Both owe their origin, their life, their all, to a covenant God entered into with them. Long before the word covenant came to express God's unique concern for man, indeed, a special tie between them, it referred to man's business with man. The business might be in the realm of politics, trade, or affection; in any case, covenant was first a social and only later a religious term. It still denotes certain human partnerships but its highest service is to bespeak the spiritual reality Scripture proclaims on most of its pages even when not naming it.

THE COVENANT OF PREDILECTION

The origin of *berit*, the Hebrew word for covenant, is uncertain. Various suggestions have been made; among others, that it is related to words meaning "bond," "fetter," "cut," or "meal." In the last two cases, the name would derive from the rites accompanying the conclusion of a covenant. Whatever its etymology, a covenant between men is a kind of brotherhood, an association of mutuality, which imposes on its partners rights and obligations, and rewards them with the gift of peace.

THE SACREDNESS OF COVENANTS A covenant may be entered into freely or be forced by one partner upon another, by the victor on the vanquished, for instance. Thus the pact does not necessarily put its contractors on a par with one another. At times, however, it is able to turn unequals into equals, as happened in the case of Jonathan, the royal prince, and David, the former shepherd boy. Jonathan loved David as dearly as his own life; he clad him in his own cloak, gave him his armor, sword, bow, and girdle—integral parts of his person, as it were—so as to fuse the two into one, thus making them inseparable. (1 Sm 18,3f) Whether the covenant was one between friends or former enemies, between husband and wife, between tribes that wished to draw closer, rulers who wanted to be allies, or neighbors who sought to live in harmony with one another, the contract was always sacred. God was its witness. (Gn 31,44)

As a sacred agreement, the conclusion of a covenant demanded a certain solemnity. The partners might pledge their loyalty by a handshake, a kiss, the offering of gifts, or the erection of a memorial: the planting of a tree or the gathering of stones into a heap. As the living timber, so the simple monument reminded the partners, again and again, of their common destiny. The covenanters might go further and seal their accord by dipping their hands jointly into a bowl of blood, by eating salt together, or by a common meal—all of them signs of their unity, indeed, instruments effecting it. The most venerable rite of all seems to have been for the confederates to walk between the halves of one or more animals. This gesture had the power of imprecation: Let the betrayer suffer the same fate as the animal victims; may he die a violent death.

GOD'S COVENANT WITH ISRAEL Covenants have been concluded throughout human history and are thus common to every age and place. God's covenant with Israel, however, was unique. It was the heart of Israel's existence. Indeed, by the second century B.C., "covenant" had become a synonym for Israel's way and worship. (Dn 11,22.28.30.32) Wherever we find nations other than Israel bound by a treaty to one god or another, these treaties in no way ruled and transformed their lives. Quite often, the tribes or nations of the Near East regarded the gods of their physical parents and themselves as being of the same race and stock as their progenitors. Israel's bond with Yahweh not only lacked the naïveté as well as the conceit of a natural bond—it was a supernatural reality. True, there were times when many in Israel suffered illusions of grandeur, when they were tempted to think of Israel as an answer to God's needs, as a royal heir well-adorned, indispensable to his father and thus safe in his position. Whenever such misapprehensions arose, they were shattered by God's spokesmen. For the concept of the chosen people has nothing to do with the nationalistic dream of inborn superiority; in fact, it is the very opposite of a "master race." Originator and Master of the covenant, God did ennoble Israel, but all her nobility is really his.

In civic as well as political life, no treaty is valid unless all contracting parties sign their names to the document. As Scripture relates the "signing" of the covenant—that is, the rites accompanying it—its authentication differed from the norm; only one partner ratified it. Instead of God *and* Israel passing between the two rows of halved animals, only God, or rather the symbols of his majesty, moved through: first a smoking oven which cast the place in an impenetrable mist, and then a fiery torch which pierced it with the radiance of his love. (Gn 15,17) Again, when at Sinai the covenant between the Lord and his people was confirmed, it was not Moses, as God's vicar, *and* the elders, as the people's representatives, who dipped their hands into a vessel of blood—Moses alone took the blood of sacrifice and sprinkled it over the assembly, saying: "This is the blood of the covenant which the Lord now makes with you. . . ." (Ex 24,8) [1]

THE LAW OF DESCENT   The terminology of the covenant, too, is perfect evidence that it was not ancient Israel who discovered a transcendent religion, who designed a sacred road to God, rather that she received a light her own genius could never have kindled. Nowhere does Scripture say that Israel made a covenant with the Lord. It is always he who makes, concludes, or establishes the bond. It is he who grants, decrees, even enjoins it. If someone should ask why God chose Israel and no other nation, the answer is simply because he loved her. If someone should press further, why did he love *her,* the answer would again be because he *loved* her. There is no other answer, no other reason, for love is its own reason.

The ancient Hebrews had little about them that was remarkable. They were not creators of a great culture but the product of one. They were not powerful either. Had there been a council of nations in those days, the voice of the Hebrews would hardly have been heard. Least of all, were they paragons of virtue. They were warned: "Do not say to yourselves, 'It is because of my rectitude that the Lord has brought me in to possess [the land promised to the fathers]. . . .' No, it is not because of your merits or the integrity of your

48

[1] Because this is a treatment of the nature of the covenant rather than of its several stages in the history of salvation, the successive covenants and covenant renewals recorded in Scripture are not dealt with. On the covenant with Noa, see Gn 9,8–17; on that with Abraham, Gn 15,7–20; on the Sinaitic covenant, Ex 19; 20; 24. On the special covenant with David and his house, see 2 Sm 7,8–16; 23,5. On the covenant renewal under Josia, see 2 Kgs 23,3; on that under Ezra and Nehemia, Neh 9; 10.

heart . . . that the Lord, your God, is giving you this good land to possess, for you are a stiff-necked people." (Dt 9,4ff) It is hard enough to grasp that they were chosen without regard for merit, virtue, or uprightness; harder still to comprehend that God adopted them, despite their stubbornness. Could it be that they are a paradigmatic people, a mirror, a lesson to all? Could it be that through them God wishes to bring home to men everywhere that whenever they are chosen, it is not their doing but the Lord's? To the Israel of old, he could have said what he says to every redeemed man: I have not loved you because you are lovable; rather, in loving you I made you lovable.

Obviously, the God who created a world vast and abundant cannot be moved by number or size. On the contrary, he is drawn to the insignificant and the weak: "It was not because you are the largest of all nations, that the Lord set his heart on you and chose you, for you are really the smallest of all nations. It was because the Lord loved you. . . ." (Dt 7,7f) What is the explanation of God's strange choice? "Like unto like," it seems, is part of nature's way. Society is largely ruled by a similar principle: "The mighty join the mighty; the dependent stay with the dependent." Such is the world of creatures. God's salvific law, however, is that of condescension.

Of the host of galaxies that fill the cosmos, he singled out our Milky Way; of all its solar systems, one cosmically quite unimportant; of all the sun's planets, the limited earth; and of the many tribes that peopled the earth, Israel, a band of slaves just escaped from its despot. Again, in the fullness of time, when grace was to appear in person and the covenant to be made new and wide to receive all mankind, his eyes fell upon no other land than that of Israel, a hated province of the Roman Empire, on no other town than Bethlehem, one of the tiniest in Juda (Mt 2,6; Mi 5,1), on no other maiden than Mary, one of the humble and poor in Israel. (Lk 1,46–55) God's work of redemption is like the ocean bending down to a drop of rain. In sum, his creative as well as his salvific design is one of "descent," to use an image of the physical world.[2] "The entire history of Israel is an adventure of love" (Jacques Guillet), her election the fruit of grace.

THE BOND OF GRACE

In an article on the covenant, the English scholar Norman H. Snaith writes: "The idea of grace more than any other idea binds the two Testaments together into a complete whole, for the Bible is the story of the saving work of God, that is, of the grace of God. Without grace, there would never have been any chosen people, any story to tell at all." (Alan Richardson, ed., *A Theological Word Book of the Bible* [New York: Macmillan, 1962], p. 101) On the other hand, Guillet holds that "if there is one reality which characterizes the Christian religion and distinguishes it from the Old Dispensation it is surely grace." (Jacques Guillet, ed., *Themes of the Bible* [Notre Dame, Indiana: Fides, 1961], p. 20)

49

---

[2] Once the law of descent is understood, the often raised question, whether or not the discovery of intelligent beings on other planets or worlds would be a mortal blow to man's dignity, indeed, to the claims of Christ and his Church, is one that cannot disturb a man of faith.

The two views seem to contradict one another, but do they? Guillet himself continues: "St. Paul opposes the reign of grace to that of the Law." (Cf. Rom 6,14f.) In doing so, the apostle certainly did not wish to imply that divine grace was not operative in the Ancient Dispensation, rather that in the New a Christian should really have no need of the constraint of the Law, not only of the Mosaic law but of any law. He should be driven by the love of Christ, not as an outer force but as the energy of the inner man; he should be propelled, as it were, into goodness by the promptings of the Holy Spirit and thus do God's will gladly and generously, even with the freshness and spontaneity that becomes a child of God.

Grace was at work in the history of Israel. Though it was like a seedling growing toward its full height in Christ; though as God's gift it had not reached the dimensions Jesus' life, death, and rising gave it; though its understanding was in flux like that of all key words of Scripture, still it was there. Grace was there because God was there, and he is ever the God of graciousness. Grace was there because the Law was ordained toward Christ, a tutor to conduct Israel to him (Gal 3,24): As every goal is the formative principle of the process leading toward it, so Christ's grace inspired the men of old even though he had not yet come in the flesh.

THE GRATUITY OF GRACE   The Old Testament does not have a single comprehensive word for God's graciousness, rather does it express the several aspects of grace by a variety of words. There is first *chen*, "favor," which derives from the verb *chanan* meaning "to bend down in order to look at someone," "to look benignly upon another." *Chen*, then, is the benevolence of a superior, his special inclination toward one of his subjects, the affection that makes him willing to grant the unclaimable and undeserved. Hence, when applied to God, *chen* proclaims the gratuity of his gift. As did the remnant of Israel's early wanderings, so another remnant of captives, having escaped the Babylonian sword, "found favor in the desert." (Jer 31,2) The penitential psalm whose beginning we usually translate: "Have mercy on me, O God," really begs God's "favor," resting its appeal, above all, on his compassion and covenant love. (Ps 50[51]3) Thus the psalter's frequent use of the sister words "merciful and gracious." (Pss 102[103]8; 144[145]8)

Since divine favor is neither the whim of a potentate nor the crumb from a rich man's table, Moses did not hesitate to remind God of his loving choice. Anxious to know whether God's gracious company would sustain him and the people throughout their desert march, Moses recalled their intimacy with bold tenderness. "You have said: 'I called you by name. . . . You have found favor with me!'" (Ex 33,12) In answer to Moses' plea, the Lord promised his continued guidance, not without adding that he would favor whom he would favor, show grace and mercy according to his good pleasure. (Ex 33,19) For his favors are free, unearned; they are gifts of love.

There is no better proof for the incipient reign of grace in the Ancient Dispensation than the Aaronic blessing. Out of a long procession of rules and laws, there greets the reader a blessing which for the Christian has lost none of its loveliness, vigor, and significance:

The Lord bless you and keep you!
The Lord let his face shine upon you, and show you his favor!
The Lord turn his [loving] face to you and grant you peace!
(Nm 6,24ff)

GRACE AHEAD OF MAN   Another aspect of grace is covered by the word *ahabah*, "love," love, that is, of every kind: of oneself, of food, sleep, hunger, or wisdom. In a general manner, it is also applied to God, to his love of justice or of Jerusalem, for example. But, as Snaith has shown, *ahabah* is sometimes used in a special sense. Take God's utterance which seems radically to deny his mercy: "I loved Jacob, but hated Esau." (Mal 1,3; Rom 9,13) The Hebrew delight in contrast makes this a hard sentence, one not easy to bear; to a Western mind, it taints the Lord with capricious fondness and hostility. If the saying is read, however, with a biblical mentality, it means: "For my elective, my salvific purpose, I chose Jacob but bypassed Esau." Again, the Lord "set his heart" on Israel; because he loved her, he broke the yoke the Egyptians laid upon her and made her walk erect. (Lv 26,13) This, his work, is *ahabah* which, when used in conjunction with the covenant, means "election-love." (Norman H. Snaith, *The Distinctive Ideas of the Old Testament* [London: Epworth, 1944], pp. 131-42)

Osea's utterances are proof of this particular meaning. He ascribes God's continued preoccupation with Israel, his spoiled and ungrateful child, to the Lord's incomprehensible predilection. How he held his son in tight embrace, how he taught him the first steps that would make him grow into a man! There was nothing God had not tried:

I drew them with human cords,
    with bands of love.
(Os 11,4)

Most likely, "human cords" refer to the gentle and selfless ties of a parent while "bands of love" stand for the ropes of *ahabah*. Another prophet, Jeremia, announces that with *ahabat 'olam*, "with everlasting love," will the Lord bring home the chosen remnant of exiles their captors have left alive. Men, some blind, some worn, will yet shout their glad hosannas, and maidens will dance in the streets because life in an alien land has come to an end. (Jer 31,2ff)

There is nothing "matter-of-course" about the Lord's love:

Think! The heavens, even the highest heavens, belong to the Lord,
your God, as well as the earth and everything on it. Yet in his love
for your fathers the Lord was so attached to them as to choose you,
their descendants, in preference to all other peoples. (Dt 10,14f)

His love is a marvel, for he to whom all things belong could not have gained anything by the special love he gave to, and sometimes wasted on, Israel.[3] This,

51

---

[3] Lest a Christian become the victim of self-righteousness, he may not point at Israel's frequent lack of response without recalling the same want within the Christian world and, above all, within himself. John XXIII, pope of evangelical love, confessed

then, is the greatness of *ahabah:* God's love knows no "must." Israel's case, however, was exactly the opposite, and so is that of every man; both are bound to love God with all their heart, soul, and might. (Dt 6,5) Before God's sovereignty, so different from man's dutiful love, the prophets stood in awe. They thundered at their people because of its infidelities, yet the thought of him made them sing:

> In his love and pity
> he himself redeemed them,
> Lifting them and carrying them
> in the days of old.
>
> (Is 63,9)

So praised one prophet, while another looked toward the messianic future, when the Lord, a mighty Savior, would again rejoice over Israel and renew her in his love. (So 3,17)

ENDURING LOVE   There are still other words that reveal in one way or another the God of grace. There is *rachamim,* for instance, "compassion" or "pity"—an interesting word because it derives from the Hebrew *rechem,* "womb," and thus connotes brotherhood, the tender feeling among those born of the same womb. This makes *rachamim,* when used of God, an almost incarnational word. Then there is *emet,* God's all-inclusive fidelity and, in particular, his faithfulness toward the covenant. (Is 49,7)

The word that excels all others is *chesed.* Generally, it is rendered as "kindness," "mercy," or "loving-kindness," but no single word can do it justice. The sacred writers outdo themselves in praise of its greatness. Momentarily languishing in a parched and waterless land, as it were, and thus athirst for God, the psalmist hails *chesed*—the Lord's merciful grace—as "a greater good than life." (Ps 62[63]4) So rich is it that men can hide under its shadow and be safe, another psalmist finds. He rejoices in God's *chesed,* the kindness, the sympathy and solidarity with men, that makes the Lord look upon the distressed weighed down by their misery, look upon their straits, their sore plight. The psalmist's trust has no limit. Knowing that his destiny is in the Lord's hands, he safely expects deliverance through God's *chesed,* through his "sure love." It is precious; it fills the heavens, covers the earth, gives life to beast, and light to men. (Ps 35[36]6–10)

Chesed is not only the joy of those pleading before God—it is his own delight. (Mi 7,18) It is "with him," his companion in his dealings with men: the grace that redeems, the love that never fails. (Ps 129[130]7) The unwavering love Hebrew men called *chesed* is his, as power is his: They are his nature. (Ps 61[62]13) Thus Israel can repeat and repeat:

52

in his 1962 Christmas message to the world that he trembled at the thought of Christ's goodness taking "pity on the miseries of a world . . . which, after twenty centuries of history, is still far from answering his invitation with a full and generous response." (Cf. *The Pope Speaks,* viii, 4 [1963], p. 355.)

> O my strength! your praise will I sing;
> for you, O God, are my stronghold,
> my gracious God!
> (Ps 58[59]18)

Frequently, God's *chesed* and his covenant with Israel are mentioned together. The Lord stands by his covenant if those he lovingly chose do not forsake him. (Dt 7,9) But his fidelity transcends that of man. He does not abandon his covenant-love for Israel even when she shows herself unworthy: In his *chesed,* his clemency, he casts her sins to the bottom of the ocean and upholds the oath he has sworn to the fathers. (Mi 7,19f)

> Though the mountains leave their place
> and the hills be shaken,
> My love [*chesed*] shall never leave you
> nor my covenant of peace be shaken,
> says the Lord, who has mercy on you.
> (Is 54,10)

When reading words like these, one can understand Snaith's suggestion that *chesed* be always rendered as covenant-love. Though covenant-love is, at times, the most appropriate translation, its exclusive use would not be precise. No doubt, *chesed* is the sure love of the unchanging God, but the love between him and his people is not one between peers. It is the love between the Chooser and the chosen, the Strong and the weak. Hence it often means goodness or kindness, pity or mercy, indeed, grace. "Enduring love," then, might best express the two poles of *chesed:* steadfastness and forbearance.

THE SEEDS OF CHRISTIAN TEACHING   It has been pointed out before in this book that the Scriptures offer no systematic treatises. Hence, none can be found there on grace. Yet, if one combines all that is implied by *chen, ahabah, chesed,* and other key words, one discovers the essential elements of the Christian teaching on grace: the gratuity of God's love; the sovereign, unfettered way of his choice; the power that goes before, with, and behind us; the divine aid that precedes and perfects our actions. Though the words of the Church's thanksgiving after Mass are her own, their seeds were sown in the days of the Ancient Dispensation. "Lord, we pray you let our doings be prompted by your inspiration and furthered by your help, so that every prayer and work of ours may begin from you, and through you be accomplished."

GOD'S PEOPLE

53

Once the lower instincts have become man's whole life, he turns the world into a moral jungle: Lust for power will make tribe battle tribe; greed or self-preservation—be it real, be it imagined—will tempt man to treat his fellow with the ferocity of a wolf.[4] It was in a world of warring nations that Israel was placed—not without her own involvement in cruel battles—for a non-war service. Ill-equipped though she seemed, still, she was given a task only God could give: to be the instrument of his Spirit and the custodian of his revelation. She was to be a witness to the nations and a prophet. (Is 43,10; St. Aug., *Against Faustus*, xiii,4) Encircled by idolators, she was yet chosen to be the worshipper of the true God. Though her own impulse and the example of her neighbors often tempted her to do as others do, she was called to be the imitator of his ways.

CHOSEN FOR OTHERS   In the realm of matter and of our daily affairs, one man's gain is another man's loss. In the realm of grace, this adamantine rule gives way to its opposite: One man's gain is the gain of many others. Hence, lavish as Scripture is in hailing Israel as God's very own people, his abode, his heritage (Ex 6,7; Lv 26,11; Dt 9,26), it insists that her singling out was not for her own sake but for that of all mankind. "Ever present in your midst, I will be your God, and you will be my people," the Lord pledged. (Lv 26,12) "If you hearken to my voice and keep my covenant," he promised, "you shall be my special possession, dearer to me than all other people, though all the earth is mine." (Ex 19,5)

The importance of the clause "all the earth is mine" can hardly be overstated. Not only does it imply that God's choice was free and unguided, it also proclaims him as the God of all men, their Sovereign as well as their Provider. Israel was thus chosen as *pars pro toto,* as a portion benefiting the whole. Her role was a priestly one: She was to be a people sacred to him, consecrated to his service, indeed, "a kingdom of priests, a holy nation." (Dt 7,6; 14,2; Ex 19,6) Evidently, her priesthood was not an end in itself. Priests are set apart, not in order to remain aloof but rather to be free for service to the faithful. Malachia calls the priest "messenger of the Lord of hosts" (Mal 2,7), while the author of Hebrews says of the high priest that, taken from among men, he is appointed on their behalf to represent them in their dealings with God. (Heb 5,1) So it was with Israel. Dwelling at the crossroads of empires, she was made God's people, not to cling to the honor but to prepare the day when "his people" would be the ingathering of men and women from every nation, when the corners of the earth would be joined in one spirit, when the *kehal Yahweh* would become the *Ecclesia toû Theoû,* the assembly of God in Christ, the Church.

The division of mankind into clans, countries, and nations bears the divine seal. Such is clearly the meaning of the table of nations (Gn 10), in whose manifoldness the sacred writer sees the evidence of God's creative hand and the fulfillment of his injunction to fruitfulness and increase. (Gn 9,1) The "Song of Moses" has the Most High assign to the nations their heritage, their homes, and

---

[4] An ancient Roman proverb says: *Homo homini lupus,* "Man is a wolf to man." It has often been used to dramatize the Darwinian "struggle for life" as if that struggle alone moved human history. In his "Comedy of Asses," the Roman poet Plautus changed the saying to: *Lupus est homo homini, non homo, quom qualis sit non novit,* "Man is no man but a wolf to a stranger." Still another version, and no doubt the best, is that of Erasmus of Rotterdam: *Homo homini aut deus aut lupus,* "Man is to man, either a god or a wolf," that is, the imitator of God or of beasts.

54

fix their boundaries. (Dt 32,8) The order of peoples is his work but not their disorder, their dissensions, as portrayed by the tower and city of Babel—a tower and city built by men in the presumption that they could maintain unity among themselves by the mere means of civilization, that they could "go it alone." Because of their *hýbris,* God confused their speech, turned it into "babble," and scattered them over the earth so that they could no longer find each other. (Gn 11,1–9)

THE MEDIATOR PEOPLE   By telling the story of Abraham's call to become the father of a people especially blessed, to be, moreover, a blessing to all nations (Gn 12,1ff), the Old Testament shows anew that God's covenant with the patriarchs and their descendants was only the glorious prologue to a more glorious embrace: The special covenant was to be transformed into a universal one, the exclusive into the all-inclusive. As a matter of fact, Israel, God's special possession, was not shut to non-Israelites; it was open to all who were ready to share her faith and life. Moses' foreign wife (Nm 12,1), Ruth the Moabite, and thousands of others who had come to rest under the wings of Yahweh (Ru 2,12), were the prototypes of millions who sought and seek refuge in the Church, the Israel reborn through the word and blood of Christ.

Thus the New Testament writers, and following them the fathers and doctors of the Church, have applied to the Church some of the great appellations by which the Israel of old was called, such as God's "vineyard," his "spouse," or his "flock." [5] They have done so gladly and with gratitude to the Lord. With many other signs, this transference proclaims the unbroken history of salvation. In God's plan, the chosen people of old is the harbinger of things-to-come:

It is a "kingdom of priests" (Ex 19,6), in which God reigns over subjects pledged to his service. Worship, the covenant's ultimate purpose, also shows the function Israel fulfills toward the other nations. Witness to them of the only God (Is 44,8), Israel is the mediator-people through which the bond between God and the whole of mankind will be renewed so that the praise of the entire earth will mount toward him (Is 45,14f.23f) and all nations share in his blessing. (Gn 12,3; Jer 4,2; Sir 44,21) (Pierre Grelot in *Vocabulaire de théologie biblique,* col. 817)

WALKING IN HIS WAYS   The covenant is at once gift and obligation. To be God's people means fully to accept his will. "Listen to my voice . . . and you shall be my people," God pleaded through the mouth of Jeremia (7,23), as he had done before through others. Only if the children of Israel obey their Lord will they remain his treasured possession. (Ex 19,5) When they became his own, did they not vow "to walk in his ways and observe his statutes, commandments and decrees"? (Dt 26,17) So much was obedience the task and test of the chosen people that "to keep the covenant"

55

---

[5] Is 5,1–7; Jer 2,21; Ps 79[80]9; Ct 4,8ff.12; Os 2,21f; Ez 6,8–14; Ps 94[95]7.

meant simply "to keep the commandments." Several laws that follow the promulgation of the Decalogue—laws that govern mainly a wide range of social duties from restitution to truthfulness and compassion (Ex 21–23) —are given the solemn name "the Book of the Covenant." (Ex 24,7) Again, before the Israelites left the site where they had been shown God's goodness but had sinned in dancing before the calf-idol, the two stone tablets on which the ten commandments were inscribed were put as reminder and warning into a wooden ark: "the Ark of the Covenant of the Lord." (Dt 10,1–8) In some psalms, "covenant" is the poetic counterpart of "precepts" or "decrees." (Pss 102[103]18; 131[132]12. The pairing of lines in a verse, called parallelism, is an original element of Hebrew poetry that serves the rhythmic beauty and, at the same time, stresses a given thought.) Thus "covenant" assumed the meaning of *torah*, God's instruction, his law.

It would be a grave misunderstanding, however, were we to mistake observance of the Law for a performance that does not engage the heart. A legalism forgetting that without love nothing avails was an aberration among Jews as it it is among Christians. The mere carrying out of rules is a relatively easy task. The great demand made on Israel, however, required more than natural courage: She was summoned to walk in the ways of the Lord with awesome fear, follow his paths in unlimited devotion, tread in his footsteps, and hold fast to him with faithful affection. (Dt 8,6; 10,12; 11,22)

An extraordinary feature may make still clearer what kind of law was given to Israel, and what kind of obedience was expected of her. The so-called Holiness-Code (Lv 17–26), compiled around 700 B.C., contains a variety of regulations. There are those on the use of blood, the right ordering of sex, the requirements and impediments of the priesthood, and others, few of them rising to great heights. Near the beginning of the Code, however, stands this imperative to the community of Israel: "Be holy, for I, the Lord, your God, am holy." (Lv 19,2) This seems to demand the impossible, it is like asking a worm to fly like an eagle. The command, nonetheless, is without restriction.

Immediately after this overwhelming behest, the Code of Holiness bids the community, among other things, not to gather stray ears of grain at harvest time or grapes fallen to the ground, but to leave them for the poor and the alien; not to steal or lie, not to defraud or withhold wages; not to insult the deaf or put a stumbling block in front of the blind; not to render partial judgment, be it in favor of the poor or the rich; not to hate or bear a grudge in one's heart, rather to love one's neighbor; to honor the aged and treat an alien like a native born. (Lv 19,9–18.33f) Significant though these latter rules are, breathing as they do the spirit of solidarity and kindness, this is not their mark of singularity. Rather is it that each one ends with the majestic affirmation: *Ani Yahweh*, "I am Yahweh," "I am the Lord," or "I am the Lord your God."

This refrain-like affirmation is to show that God is the source of all morality, the fount of all goodness. More than that, it told Israel that every

56

member of God's people had to be kind, faithful, honest, without guile and deceit because the Lord was thus, and as his people they had to be like him. To imitate God was every Israelite's task. The prophet Michea put the *imitatio Dei* expected of Israel into a saying of special beauty:

> You have been told, O man, what is good,
> and what the Lord requires of you:
> Only to do the right and to love goodness,
> and to walk humbly with your God.
>
> (Mi 6,8)

"Goodness" in the line before last is the translation of *chesed*. According to Professor Harold H. Rowley, *chesed* is "of the essence of God's heart. . . . The qualities of loyalty, love, and grace are all included in the rich amalgam of this word." (*The Rediscovery of the Old Testament* [Philadelphia: Westminster, 1946], pp. 155f) It is the spirit God showed the children of Israel throughout their history, which they were bound, therefore, to manifest toward one another. Unless they wished to betray his love, their ways had to reflect *his*. In their humble walk with him, they were to show toward their kinsmen, to whom they were tied not only by blood but by grace, a warm and gracious spirit resembling the spirit of Yahweh. As he took the initiative and turned to them, so they had to turn toward their fellows: not shrink from any service, not wait till it was asked but offer it the way the Lord offered his gifts. Utterance upon utterance addressed by Christ to his people—first to those of his own flesh, then to those willing to accept his tidings—sought to enforce and widen this spirit. For he came to give it freshness, vigor, and a scope that forgets no one.

The imperative, "Be holy, for I, the Lord your God, am holy," led toward Christ's "Be perfect, as your heavenly Father is perfect" (Mt 5,48), and the exhortation to walk with God found its fulfillment in Jesus' call: "Come, follow me!" (Mk 1,17) The command to imitate God's holiness formed part of a code; Christ's summons to imitate divine perfection, however, belongs to that new proclamation which seeks to set the disciples on fire and awaken hearts to the Spirit's breath. Again, the ancient Israelite was told to walk with the unseen God; the disciples, in turn, are asked to walk with him who is the perfect Image of the Father. (Jn 12,45; 14,9)

CHANTERS BEFORE THE LORD   To celebrate Israel's restoration after her fifty years in exile, the Second Isaia pleads for a cosmic liturgy. He tells the sea to roar and the wilderness to cry out; he asks the heavens to sing and the earth, with its mountains and forests, to shout for joy. (Is 42,10ff; 44,23) Set between these pleas for a resounding oratorio sung by the whole of creation is God's description of Israel as

57

> The people whom I formed for myself,
> that they might announce my praise.
>
> (Is 43,21)

One of Israel's principal means for rendering honor to God was the psalms. Though the psalter may not have been given its present form till about 200 B.C., many individual psalms were composed long before, some three or three and a half centuries earlier, others in the era of the kings, still others even as far back as David's time. The book of Psalms contains a variety of genres: hymns of praise; songs of thanksgiving, communal or individual; supplications or laments of the people or of a single sufferer, often voicing confidence in the Lord or ending with an expression of gratitude. There are still others: "the Songs of Sion," exalting the holy city, some of them looking toward Yahweh's universal reign; the "Royal Psalms," mostly salutations of the ruling king or prayers and thanksgivings on his behalf.

Though the Royal Psalms were written for specific occasions, they were not riveted to these happenings so firmly that their significance could not outlast the moments that inspired their composition. Here as elsewhere, the present anticipated the future: The reigning king was only the shadow of the great King-to-come, the Anointed *par excellence,* the Blessed One of the Lord. (Ps 117[118]26; Mt 21,9) The psalter itself does not classify the various psalms; in one instance, it calls them all "prayers." (Ps 71[72]20) The name generally given it by Jewish tradition—its different genres notwithstanding—is *tehillim,* the book of divine praisings. Whoever was responsible for this designation may have named the entire book after its loftiest parts. Or, he may have held that all the psalms sing God's glory, whether they offer him the fragrance of praise or bring to him, their Healer, the stench of human misery.

True men of prayer, the authors of the psalms craved no fame and thus remain unknown. If David's name is mentioned in the headings of seventy-three psalms, this need not be taken as a claim of his actual authorship. Still, as initiator and promoter of sacred song in Israel's public worship, he was "godfather" to those and all other psalms. He is said to have been the one who appointed and trained the men who were to glorify the Lord with harp, lyre, cymbal, trumpet, and chant. (1 Chr 16,4–36; 25,1–7) A poet, he was also a fool for God. (2 Sm 1,17–27; cf. 1 Cor 3,18f; 4,10.) When the Ark of the Covenant had been rescued from Israel's enemies and brought into his keep, he—the king—was not ashamed to dance before all the people to the accompaniment of trumpets, in honor of the Lord. (2 Sm 6,14ff)

In the psalms, every emotion surges forth; the one that seems to leap highest is joy in the Lord, joy in the God who himself rejoices in his works. (Ps 103[104]31–34) This is why music played an essential part in Israel's worship. The great feasts as well as the daily sacrifices were not silent gatherings of individual worshippers concerned with nothing but their own intentions. They were acts of the community. Here was the flock of Yahweh, the house of Jacob spelling out the Lord's glory; here were the sons of Sion, the members of the covenant, each one praising and pleading in the midst of the assembly. To their voices was joined the melody of string, wind, and percussion instruments. But this was not all: Because the worshipping community was alive, there was movement, rhythmic movement. The pilgrims to Jerusalem approached the Temple gates in eager procession; in awe and delight, they walked around the altar; in humble prostration, they fell to the ground; they clapped their hands and danced, overpowered by the happiness of being in the Lord's presence. Still, Israel knew that all her singing and leaping, all her lyric prayer could not match his greatness. (Sir. 43,29–35)

Though we can say only of a few psalms at what hour, service, or feast they were sung, there can be no doubt that the psalter served as the hymnbook of the second Temple. This is not to say that Solomon's Temple and the tabernacle of old did not resound with melody, with cries of entreaty, tributes of gratitude, and hymns of adoration. Some of the psalms must have been also on the lips of individual worshippers, at times not determined by the set order of public ceremonies. What better evidence could there be than three of the last words of Jesus? In the moment of deepest abandonment which, at the same time, was the greatest liturgical hour ever, he spoke with words "borrowed" from the psalter. (Pss 21[22]2.15f; 30[31]6) No wonder that the Church made it her book of hours, indeed, that she wove the psalms into all her liturgical functions. She did not drop as much as a single line. She left standing even the curses the persecuted of old hurled at their tormentors.[6]

These imprecations were the outcries of men oppressed whose faith, however, was unshaken and whose clamor for justice was a cutting wind. If they were vindictive, it was because of their deep sensitivity toward right and wrong, a sensitivity not common among their pagan neighbors. Yet, it was a sensitivity "unbaptized," and "uncrucified." The freedom of the children of God, the inner detachment from hostile reactions so quick to rise in the hearts of men, had not yet been proclaimed from the mount of beatitudes nor had it been lived on Golgotha, the mount of forgiveness. It would be a denial of Christ's significance to expect that men prior to his coming could in every way have lived as Christians ought—but seldom do. In any case, the vengeful demands that the enemy be punished may benefit the Christian worshipper if they remind him that, left to himself, he, too, may be the victim of his anger. In the hour of persecution, his own heart may shout for vengeance unless he has labored, day by day, to be one with his Father in heaven, who makes his sun rise on good and bad alike (Mt 5,45), and to live by Christ's admonition: "Love your enemies, do good to those who hate you." (Mt 5,44)

---

[6] See Pss 34[35]1–8; 57[58]7–11; 68[69]23–29; 78[79]6; 82[83]14–19; 108[109] 6–15; 136[137]7ff; 139[140]9ff. In reading these prayers for vengeance, one must keep in mind the excessiveness of language that is natural to the men of the Near East. One would misunderstand them were one to take literally the request, for instance, that God "smash [the] teeth [of the wicked] in their mouths" or the assurance that "the just man . . . shall bathe his feet in the blood of the wicked." (Ps 57[58]7.11) Because Hebrew speech is vivid, passionate, even extravagant, it is certainly no worse than the often proud restraint of "stoics" or the understatement of Anglo-Saxons. Is it not, perhaps, more human? Israel's God is an impassioned God, and only impassioned men could be the bearers of his revelation. That their passion at times burst into curses is part of the price we must pay for a slowly unfolding message of love. Again, the Hebrew manner of thought is concrete and not given to distinctions, hence the psalmists often failed to distinguish between sinners and their sins. As men trying with all their might to serve God, the singers of the psalms were apt to identify themselves with God and thus consider enemies who hated them, God's servants, as enemies of the Lord. The Christian world has not always escaped this pitfall. Though Christ may declare his oneness with those who are persecuted for his sake (Ac 9,5; 22,4f.7f), the persecuted disciple must always remain aware of the distance between himself and his Master. On the whole problem, see St. Thomas, $S.Th.$, 2^a2^{ae}, 25,6.

CHRIST AND THE PSALTER   St. Augustine calls Christ *iste cantator,* "this unique Singer." (*Sermon on Ps 122*) From the days of his childhood, he was taught the songs of Israel. The first one to initiate him into the art of praise could have been none other than Mary, his earliest and matchless teacher in the things of acquired human knowledge. At times, she may have chanted the psalms to the accompaniment of a small harp till his lips moved with hers. From then on, and all through his manhood, Israel's hymns often gladdened his heart or made it tremble because of the hardships men must bear.

When at the age of twelve, he accompanied his mother and Joseph, his father by law and by love, on their paschal pilgrimage to Jerusalem (Lk 2,41f), he no doubt greeted the holy city as did the whole caravan:

> I rejoiced because they said to me,
> "We will go up to the house of the Lord."
> (Ps 121[122]1)

No doubt, he joined in the exclamation:

> How lovely is your dwelling place,
> O Lord of hosts!
> (Ps 83[84]2)

With the other wayfarers, he must have chanted the "pilgrim songs," songs of ascent to Mount Sion. (Pss 119[120]–133[134]) At the gathering of his family for the celebration of the Passover, and no less in the company of his disciples, he chanted with them the hymns of praise prescribed for that festive occasion.

There is one group of psalms that permits a special glimpse of Jesus' inner life: those in which the *anawim,* the poor and afflicted, pour out their hearts. Harassed by the wicked (Ps 9B[10]2), by proud braggarts, they were "a people humble and lowly . . . the remnant of Israel." (So 3,12) Though they were mocked, shamed, and maltreated, their misfortune neither weakened their faith nor lessened their love. God was their Stronghold. (Ps 9A[9]10) As the meat of sacrificial meals brought joy to the company of worshippers, so did God himself: He was their food, their portion, their cup. (Ps 15[16]5) They trusted him as a servant does his master (Ps 85[86]2), an orphan his guardian. (Ps 9B[10]14) On him, they staked all they were and had. The Lord in turn took their misery into his hands (Ps 9B[10]14), adorning them with victory. (Ps 149,4) In the man Jesus, generations of *anawim* reached their summit. In him, their trials and victories were so heightened that he did not need to follow the prophet in calling on the "humble of the earth" to seek the Lord and go after justice and humility. (So 2,3) He could simply cry out: "Learn from me, for I am meek and humble of heart." (Mt 11,29)

Not only his recital and prayer, his life, too, revealed Jesus as the

Singer of the psalter, the Interpreter and Doer of its words. What moved St. Augustine still more was that Christ, no longer the Suffering Servant but the One "seated at the right hand of God" (Col 3,1), no longer the Poor *par excellence* but the King of glory, still sings the psalms. Now he sings them with the new Israel, with and through his Church. Through St. Augustine's sermons on the psalms moves the idea of the "entire Christ": Christ, the Head, and the faithful, his body; he, the Savior, and they, the community of the saved. Even if one cannot accept every single interpretation St. Augustine gives of this or that verse, one cannot but marvel at, and aspire to, the enthusiasm that makes him so frequently speak of Christ and the Church as "two in one flesh," "two with one voice." (*On Ps 142*)

Whether it is the Head who speaks or the members, St. Augustine loves to announce: "It is Christ who speaks." Whether it is the Head who speaks or the body, it is one life, one spirit that manifests itself in the psalter. (*On Ps 74*)

> Though removed from our eyes, he is welded to us by his love. Because the total Christ is head and body, we hear in all the psalms the words of the head, but hear them in such a way that we hear also the words of the body. He did not wish to speak apart from his brethren because he did not wish to be separated from them. Thus he said: "I am with you all days, even unto the consummation of the world." (Mt 28,20) Being with us, he speaks in us, speaks of us, speaks through us. No less do we speak in him, indeed, only when we speak in him do we speak the truth. (*On Ps 61*)

Commenting on the verse, "there is no wholeness in my bones because of my sin" (Ps 37[38]4), St. Augustine asks for the sake of his hearers how the sinless Christ can pray "because of my sin." The bishop of Hippo leaves no doubt that this and similar expressions are the voice of the Lord, although the sins are those of the members of his mystical body. He rejoices in the mystery of the one body, the one tongue. Till the end of time, he holds, Christ's body will groan in pain. It will cry out to God till suffering is no more. Now, when the body cries, Christ cries, for "all men are one in Christ." (*On Pss 85 and 39*) "This Man is all men, and all men are this Man." (*On Ps 34*). In another of his sermons on the psalms, he exclaims:

> *Ascendat ergo iste cantator,* may he rise, therefore, this unique Singer. From the heart of each one of you, may this Man sing, and each one of you be that Man. Even when you speak singly, it is still this one Man who speaks since you are all one in Christ. He does not say: "To you, we lift up our eyes," rather:
>
> To you I lift up my eyes
> who are enthroned in heaven.
> (Ps 122[123]1)

61

So much is the anguish of creatures Christ's own concern, so gladly does he carry their hopes that the late Father Gelin could remark of St. Augustine's meditations on the psalms: "They throw open to us the dimensions of the Christ, the Christ who is 'the universal brother,' 'the man with a thousand hearts.'" (Albert Gelin, *La prière des psaumes* [Paris: Editions de l'Epi, 1961], p. 99)

CHAPTER FOUR

KINGDOM OF PRIESTS

"Let my people go to worship me," was the unconditional demand God sent to Egypt's king. (Ex 9,2) To hallow his name, then, was Israel's mission. Later, at the height of her unfolding history, she sought to accomplish it through an elaborate system of sacrifices. In the beginning, her rites were simple and provisional; today the altar might be built in one place, tomorrow in another. (Gn 12,8; Ex 20,24)

63

When Solomon (970–31 B.C.), in fulfillment of his father's dearest wish, erected "a house for the name of the Lord" (1 Kgs 8,18) where the Ark of the Covenant could be given a permanent home, he made a first move toward the unification of Israel's cultic life. But not until Josia (639–09 B.C.) were the numerous shrines throughout the country suppressed—many of which had become nests of idolators, of worshippers of the sun or the moon, even of practitioners of human sacrifice by fire. The Temple itself had been desecrated by the invocation of a Chanaanite god and a Phoenician goddess—Scripture has only one verdict for pagan worship in the house of the living God: abomination. Cleansed by the king, the Temple was made the one sanctuary in which the one people was to offer sacrifice to the one God. (2 Kgs 23,4–20; Dt 12,1–14)

SACRIFICES

About a hundred years later, after the trials of the Babylonian exile, the book of Leviticus compiled and codified the various sacrifices that in centuries past had, under God's guidance, come into being or taken on new shape. (Lv 1–7; 16; 17) To Western man, this intricate system of offerings seems foreign; some may even find the slaughtering of animals in the Temple, with all its bloody manipulations, repugnant. To the Jews of old, however, sacrifices were sacred things, several were even called *kodesh* [*ha-*] *kodashim,* things most holy.[1] Sacrifices were gifts acknowledging the lordship of God who himself owns the goods of which man is apt to deem himself the possessor, even though they are only loaned to him. Twice God bid his people: "No one shall appear before me empty-handed." (Ex 23,15; 34,20) The holocaust or burnt-offering, *'olah,* in which an entire animal was consumed by fire so that not even the tiniest portion could be eaten by the offerer conveyed, more than other offerings, the idea of total giving.

GOD'S PRESENCE   As the offerers expressed gratitude and submission, so they manifested the desire to enter into the presence of Yahweh. A general term for sacrifice used, for instance, in connection with some types of cereal offering, *minchah*—that is, the presentation of choice flour mixed with oil or baked in an oven—is *korban.* (Lv 2,1.4) Commonly, *korban* is rendered as "offering" or "oblation"; in later times, the word came to mean something pledged to God and thus withdrawn from ordinary use. (Mk 7,11) Its original meaning, however, was "that which is brought near." By his gift, then, the worshipper drew near the Giver of treasures, great and small. If the gift was offered in the

---

[1] In Lv 6,18, a sacrifice involving slaughter and thus the shedding of blood, without which there is no atonement, no forgiveness (Lv 17,11; Heb 9,22), is called most sacred. In rabbinical literature, however, that is in the writings composed several centuries after the destruction of the Temple and the forced abolition of its sacrifices, it is rather the bloody offerings that are considered less holy, while the unbloody ones are thought to be most holy.

right spirit, God made his presence felt—so much so that St. Paul could find no better image for God's innermost presence in the members of the New Covenant than the former place of sacrifice. "Do you not know," he asks the Corinthians, "that you [the community as well as each member] are the temple of God and that the Spirit of God dwells in you?" (1 Cor 3,16)

In the so-called peace-offering, *zebach shelamim,* the desire to be in God's presence became the desire for communion with him. After a worshipper had slaughtered an animal without blemish at the assigned place, the priests poured the blood about the altar, while the intestinal fat and some of the entrails had to be handed over to the fire on the altar so as to be turned into a flaming gift and a pleasing odor for the Lord. (Lv 3) At certain times, the peace-offering was the sacrifice of the community; most of the time, however, that of an individual or a family. Certain portions of the meat had to be presented to the priest in attendance (Lv 7,14.31–34), the rest was merrily eaten by the worshipper and his friends. God was considered the Guest at their happy gathering, their "love-feast," and they were said to eat "in the sight of the Lord." (Dt 12,18) Through this sacred meal the ties that bound the sacrificer and his companions to the God of the covenant were fastened once more.

ATONEMENT   Not the least important element in Israel's sacrificial system was atonement. In the postexilic era, if not before, all sacrifices were meant to cleanse the sinner. There was *chatt'at,* the sin-offering for trespasses unwittingly committed. Amends had to be made for them, for even involuntary sins were considered to be in need of expiation. (Lv 4,1–5,13) There was also *asham,* the guilt-offering. For dues withheld from the Temple, even inadvertently, "the penalty of the guilt must be paid to the Lord." (Lv 5,19) Again, for having denied one's neighbor a deposit, a pledge, or some stolen goods, for having intimidated or defrauded him, for having wronged him through perjury, for these and other misdeeds full restitution was required, and a fifth part of the total amount besides. Still, such reparation was not held to be sufficient: that the wrongdoer be forgiven, the priest had to make atonement for him through a guilt-offering. (Lv 5,20–26)

None of the statutes regulating the sacrifices call the animal victims substitutes for man, the sinner and sacrificer. According to some interpreters, the laying of hands upon their heads—an integral part of all bloody sacrifices (Lv 1,4; 3,2.8.13; 4,15.24.29)—implied as much. According to most exegetes, however, the imposition of hands was but a solemn declaration that a particular victim was presented to the Lord in the offerer's name; thus he pleaded for God's favor and "claimed" for himself the fruits of the sacrifice. There can be no question as to the special rite for the Day of Atonement: The hands resting on the live goat about to be chased into the wilderness spelled out most clearly that the goat was to carry the faults, transgressions, and sins of the people into the nowhere. (Lv 16,21f) Without knowing it, the scapegoat bore the people's burden and the punishment due to them; the animal was removed from the world of men so that the sinners might not be removed from the sight of God.

THE SUFFERING SERVANT   The vicarious role of the victim—only a possible interpretation of the slaughter of animals but the clear intent of driving a live goat into the desert, the place of banishment for Azazel, prince of devils—was given an altogether new quality in the Isaian vision of the Man of pain. What the animal, without wit or will, symbolized was in him reality. The goat sent into the dead wilderness was totally unaware of its function; not for an instant did it consider itself a victim and thus an instrument of reconciliation: The goat itself did nothing, everything happened to it. The Suffering Servant, however, assumes man's burdens freely. Freely, he offers his life for us, as *asham*, a guilt-offering, a sacrifice of reparation. (Is 53,10) Not only in his body but in his full humanity, he is "pierced for our offenses, crushed for our sins." (Is 53,5)

Has there ever been one to correspond to this vision except Jesus of Nazareth? His own sacrifice on the cross brought to glorious culmination the diverse offerings of the Ancient Dispensation. There could have been no happier fulfillment of the many sacrifices than to see the one make transparent what they told but dimly: God's mercy and all-embracing will to save. Not that there is any detailed correspondence between "the many" and "the one." "The many" were rituals of duty, "the one" the freely chosen climax of a sacrificial life. Still, they are related to one another as a rich painting to its light sketches, nay, as the exemplar to its copies.

There is an oracle in the book of Malachia whose meaning is much disputed among scholars. The Council of Trent, however, showed no hesitation in applying it to the sacrifice of the Mass offered in almost every land where men dwell. (D939[1742]; TCT748) Though Malachia's words may be veiled, as most prophetic utterances are, no other holy action matches his spiritual panorama better than the Mass, sacrifice of forgiveness and praise, banquet of the New Covenant and feast of God's enduring love:

> From the rising of the sun, even to its setting,
>   my name is great among the nations;
> And everywhere they bring sacrifice to my name,
>   and a pure offering;
> For great is my name among the nations,
>   says the Lord of hosts.
>
> (Mal 1,11)

SACRAMENTS

So that they would not forget that Yahweh was Lord of the land, the Israelites were required to set aside a tenth of their harvest. Their tithing also served the ministers of worship as well as the poor. (Dt 14,22–29; Nm 18,21–32) Hugh of St. Victor saw in the tithes of the Old Testament nothing less than sacraments, tokens of God's favor. (*On the Sacraments*, I,xi,4)

Though there is no agreement as to their number, it is the unanimous tradition of the Church that sacraments were an essential factor of the economy of the Old Covenant. Non-Catholic scholars, generally, do not share this view; yet, the Church holds fast to it. Not only do all major theologians speak of the sacraments of the Old Law, but two councils, those of Florence and Trent, expressly teach their existence. (D695[1310]; 845[1602]; TCT663; 666)

THE NATURE OF THE SACRAMENTS OF OLD   According to the Council of Florence, the sacraments of old differed considerably from those of the Christian era. The former did not generate grace in their recipients as do the latter, for the latter are prolongations, as it were, of the Sacrament of sacraments: God in the flesh. The ancient sacraments were gestures of God's nearness, and thus far from the presence, the embodiment, of his being in the man Jesus. Nonetheless, they prefigured the grace that was to be granted to man by Christ's coming and passion. (S.Th., 1ª2ᵃᵉ,101,4,ad 2) They were heralds. But does not the herald to some extent share in the dignity of the king he precedes? Christ has not yet accomplished his errand of mercy; still, in the providence of God, an event of such magnitude as Christ's redemptive work breaks the time barrier. It sends waves in all directions.

The former sacraments could not have been empty signs for they were divine institutions. They helped weld the people into one and strengthen the link God had forged by his covenant. Hence, they were means leading to sanctification, even though the mantle of holiness they held out was, so to speak, of heavy linen rather than fine silk, even though grace did not flow as copiously then as it does under the shepherding staff of Christ. Within the context of the Ancient Dispensation, they prepared the people, and consecrated the ministers, for divine worship. (S.Th., 1ª2ᵃᵉ,101,4) If received in the spirit required, they helped the adult members of the covenant to a life of justice and moved them to gentle trust, fervent sorrow, and genuine love. Thus, with the assistance of actual graces, the Israelites were made ready for the infusion of sanctifying grace. Strengthened by his love, they were enabled to walk with him.

In one of his articles on the sacraments of the Old Covenant, St. Thomas deals with the objection that they were but shadows of Christ. Hence they did not pertain to his body, the argument continues, and since they did not, Christ cannot be called the Head of all men. As always, St. Thomas's answer is to the point:

> The holy fathers [of the Ancient Dispensation] eagerly used the sacraments the Law prescribed, though not as realities, rather as images and shadows of things-to-come. Now, the movement that leads to an image, in so far as it is an image, is the same as the one leading to reality. . . . By observing the sacraments of the Law, therefore, the ancient fathers were borne to Christ by the same faith

67

and love by which we are brought to him. Thus the fathers of old belonged to the same body of the Church to which we belong. (S.Th., 3ᵃ,8,3, ad 3)

Pursuing this thought further, we may say that the spiritual community of Israel—the Church in the making—was itself a sacrament, a means of cleansing, sanctification, and fellowship with God. The Church made manifest at Pentecost, too, is such a sacrament, indeed, one of superabundance. Again, time or sacred history had and has sacramental quality. It was by visible events that the invisible God visited his people. It is in time, the meeting ground of God and man, that man, "with fear and trembling," works out his salvation. (Phil 2,12)

CIRCUMCISION   The greatest of the sacraments of old were circumcision and the paschal lamb. To dwell for the moment on the first: St. Gregory the Great taught that the power baptism has now among Christians was once held for those of Abraham's stock by the mystery of circumcision. (Treatise on Morals, IV,3) The Venerable Bede spoke of circumcision as offering to the men of the Law "the same aid of restorative healing against the wound of original sin" that baptism bestows on the followers of Christ. (Homily X, On the Feast of the Circumcision) Again, Hugh of St. Victor writes that the sacrament of circumcision was given to the seed of Abraham as a means of sanctification and a mark of distinction. It justified Abraham's offspring by freeing them from the debt of the first sin and singled them out from the nations so that they might remain in sacred retreat from others. Thus the strain from which Christ was born could be distinguished. (On the Sacraments, I,xii,2) Finally, St. Thomas holds that circumcision cleansed from original sin and conferred hallowing grace so that, at the allotted time, children would be admitted to that glory which is the crowning of grace. Wondrous economy! The blood of the circumcised, though powerless in itself, foreshadowed the blood that was "shed for many unto the forgiveness of sins." (Mt 26,28; cf. Heb 9.)

True, circumcision lacked many of the fruits baptism grants the Christian who is a new creature in Christ. Baptism is "the instrument of Christ's passion consummated" while circumcision was "a sign of faith in Christ's passion-to-come." (S.Th., 3ᵃ,70,4) Faith here was not that of the infant to be circumcised but the corporate faith of the covenant community with which the child was now united. It was Israel's hopeful vision of the One-to-come—which was often no more than a groping in the dark, subject to all the vicissitudes that are ever part of man's struggle in understanding God's revelation—that gave her history its push toward the future. It was also this hope-filled faith of the spiritual community that acted as "godfather" to the child who had to be wounded in the flesh so as to be healed in the spirit.

None in Israel was forsaken by God's salvific will. Newborn boys who

68

died before their circumcision as well as girls who died in their infancy might well have been justified by their parents' faith, prayers, or blessings. (S.Th., 3ª,70,4, ad 2) Older girls and women were brought to the healing and hallowing encounter with God by their personal trust and surrender, their use of other rites, their participation in Israel's feasts, in short, by all that made them do God's will.

THE SOIL OF THE CHRISTIAN SACRAMENTS   Their character as the spiritual remedies of the Old Covenant does not exhaust the significance of Israel's sacraments. They also prepared for those of the new Israel. As circumcision, a widespread rite of initiation into manhood among African, Australian, and American tribes, was taken over by the Israelites, probably from the Egyptians, and divinely transformed into the seal of the covenant, so several rites of the Ancient Dispensation served as matrix for the sacraments Christ gave to his Church. To begin with the sacrament that the Christian as wayfarer to the promised land normally receives last, there was in the Israel of old no rite like the anointing of the ill. Still, visiting the sick was held to be a godlike work: To bring them comfort was among the chosen tasks of certain pious brotherhoods. For Christ himself, healing was a precious part of his ministry; giving courage to the sick, he taught, was one of the works of love that determine a man's eternal destiny. (Mt 25,36) Oil was used for medicinal purposes (Lk 10,34); indeed, the disciples are said to have cured many of the sick by anointing them. (Mk 6,13) Certainly, all this formed the background for the sacrament of divine compassion for the ill whose prayers plead for their restoration within and without. (Jas 5,13ff)

Though the family was all-important to the ancient people of God, the wedding was, strange to say, a private affair between the two families concerned. The marriage formula used might be as simple as: "You shall be my wife" or "She is my wife, and I am her husband, from this day forever." Still, marriage was not only considered worthy of honor, it was thought of as a remainder and reminder of paradise. (Gn 2,18.21–24; 1,27f) When Malachia's contemporaries wondered why God had rejected their sacrifices, the prophet answered:

Because the Lord is witness
    between you and the wife of your youth,
With whom you have broken faith
    though she is your companion, your betrothed wife.
Did he not make one being, with flesh and spirit:
    and what does this one being seek but godly offspring?
You must then safeguard life that is your own,
    and not break faith with the wife of your youth.
For I hate divorce,
    says the Lord, the God of Israel.

(Mal 2,14ff)

69

These words, among others, spoken more than four hundred years before Christ's coming, set the atmosphere for his presence at Cana (Jn 2,1–12), for his restoration of the uniqueness of the bond between spouses (Mt 19,1–9), and for St.

Paul's vision of matrimony as the replica of Christ's mystical union with the Church. (Eph 5,21–33)

The various ablutions imposed by the Law till the coming of a new order (Heb 9,10), the public confessions, the penitential psalms, all these paved the way for the sacrament of penance. Again, the consecrations of the high priests and all other ministers of the Temple liturgy are figures of the sacrament of holy orders. (Ex 29,29; Lv 8,1–9) The laying on of hands, in particular, was in the days of the Law the means of transmitting spiritual power (Nm 27,18ff; Dt 34,9), as it is today the "matter" in the ordination of priests as well as in the consecration of bishops. On both occasions, the Church delights in looking back on the offices, ceremonies, vestments, and symbols of the Ancient Dispensation as the precursors, even the patterns of the present hierarchical order.

WASHINGS AND BAPTISM   Unique though Christian baptism is, it was not without its happy analogies, some distant, some near. The early pages of Scripture speak of Noa's rescue from the death-bringing flood (Gn 7–8), while Israel's history begins with the unharmed passage through the waters that could so easily have engulfed her. (Ex 14,10–22) Both are "types" of baptism. (A biblical type is an event or person of Israel's divinely guided history which foreshadows the Messia, messianic times, or messianic gifts.) Again, the ritual washings with which the Old Testament legislation abounds are not without significance for the sacrament that cleanses and hallows man. They were purifications from an uncleanness in no way immoral, excluding, nonetheless, the afflicted from taking part in the worship of the community. They were bound up with birth, death, and other phenomena linked mainly to life's ebb and flow. (Lv 14–15; Nm 19) There seems in these washings an intimation that life, token of God's bounty, is tainted with sin and cries, as it were, for "sister water, serviceable, selfless, beloved, and chaste." (St. Francis, *Canticle to the Most High God*) In any case, the prophetic cry: "Wash yourselves clean!" (Is 1,16), as well as the psalmist's prayer: "Wash me, and I shall be whiter than snow" (Ps 50[51]9), point to a deeply felt need for hearts that are pure. (Mt 5,8)

Though the origin and intent of the rite are not entirely clear, Jews were accustomed to baptize proselytes—men and women who had abandoned their pagan ways for a life in conformity with the Law—probably to assure ritual integrity. Jewish tradition has preserved several sayings that breathe the same spirit. One of them maintains that to stand in God's presence men must undergo baptism. In the messianic age, then, God himself will pour the waters of purification upon the people of Israel, according to the words of the prophet: "I will sprinkle pure water upon you to purify you from all your impurities, and from all the dirt of your idols I will cleanse you." (Ez 36,25) Another saying calls God "You, the *mikweh* of Israel," *mikweh* meaning hope as well as pool of immersion. The Lord was thus seen as Israel's hope and as the fountain of her purity—a perfect background for Christ's institution of the sacrament of rebirth.

Further, the community of Qumrân, whose monastery and library

70

were only recently discovered, seems to have been but a fragment of a whole "cleansing movement." Its monks had severed all links with a world they considered wicked and polluted because it did not accept their rigorous interpretation of the Law of Moses. In the midst of, and yet apart from, those who looked for a spotless spirit by following a routine of rigidity and a wealth of precepts, stood an austere and lonely man: John the Baptist. His baptism was different. It was prophetic. Prophetic, first, was the warning that to be no more than a son of Abraham by blood was useless without repentance, without the heart's unconditioned turning to God.[2] Prophetic, too, was the proclamation by word and water that God's forbearance was approaching its end; that his judgment was near; that the ax had been "laid at the root of the trees." Prophetic, above all, was the announcement that the messianic times were at hand; that the reign of God was upon the people; indeed, that One mightier than John the precursor was in their midst. He would baptize with fire and the Spirit. (Mt 3,2.9–12; Lk 3,9; Mk 1,7f)

The gospel passage still trembles with the bewilderment of the Baptist when he heard Jesus ask to be baptized as if he were part of the multitude. The expected One of Israel, pure and without stain, so identified himself with sinners that he joined their ranks at the Jordan. He had come to fulfill God's will, honor his holiness, and declare that he desired for his brethren the sinners, not doom but life abundant. Little did the Baptist realize that Jesus' baptism itself was prophetic, announcing as it did another: that of his saving death, of his own blood running down his body in order to wash the world clean. (Lk 12,50; Mk 10,38; Jn 19,34f) To sum up, the rite of baptism, the immersion in water, was waiting for Christ to use. Taking it, he breathed into it a new meaning. The baptism he demands is a sign, not merely indicative but also efficacious of his disciple's oneness with him. With him, the Christian is buried in the font; with him, he rises from there. (Col 2,12) The reborn man or woman is now part of his mystical body walking through the centuries, part of the Church, part of the new Israel; indeed, he is taken to God's bosom as a daughter or a son. (1 Cor 12,12f)

PASSOVER: THE LAMB AND THE BREAD

It was an old custom among Semitic tribes to slaughter an animal and, with its blood, spray the doorposts and the threshold of an abode, in particular of a new tent. Thus they expected to chase away the evil powers. The ancient Hebrews must have brought this usage into Egypt. Every

---

2 The members of the new Israel are in a similar danger. To be found in the registers of the Church without being a true partaker of her life profits a man nothing. Still, a tenuous link remains. At times, then, the return to the Church of a dormant or dead member may be easier than the entry of one who has spent his life outside her walls.

spring, they seem to have offered an unblemished yearling, lamb or kid, shedding its blood as a plea for the increase of their flocks and the protection of their dwellings. Hence, when the Lord God was about to shatter the stubborn will of Pharao and free his people, Moses must have evoked confidence in his kinsmen by his firm command that each family get a lamb and slaughter it. With a blood-soaked bunch of hyssop, they sprinkled the lintels and doorposts of their houses. Whatever house was thus signed was spared, "passed by," as death struck the Egyptians. (Ex 12,21-27)

As the "must" and "seem" in the preceding paragraph indicate, several statements just made, as well as several to be made in the following two sections, are hypothetical. Scholarly opinions on the origin and development of the Passover vary; the theory offered here appears to be the most plausible. Still, not a few of its assertions must remain conjectural since Scripture is not designed to satisfy our scientific curiosity. After all, its sacred writers are not "historians of religion" preoccupied with the antecedents and stages of faith and feasts. As theologians, their eyes are fixed on God's formative will and their words bear witness to his deed, to the grace shaping the events of their people's history and worship.

THE MEANING OF THE PASCHAL LAMB   It was at the vernal equinox—at the time when the old spring festival used to be held—that the Lord showed himself victorious, rescuing his people: Thus began the springtime of Israel's history, with nature serving as the backdrop for the display of God's gracious power. Through his saving deed, the primitive sacrifice obtained a new and exalted meaning, indeed, its whole character was changed. From a pastoral rite, it was turned into a *zikkaron*, a memorial, of the Exodus for all coming generations (Ex 12,14), into the anniversary of the hour when God bared his arm, showed his zeal, revealed his heart, manifested his pity and mercy. (Is 63,12.15) This was Yahweh's great feast for it recalled those wonders upon which Israel's entire life, her faith, her love were founded.

The name by which Scripture likes to call the feast is "the *Pesach* of Yahweh," "the Passover of the Lord" (Ex 12,11), usually shortened to *Pesach* or Passover. According to the biblical interpretation, *pesach* derives from the verb *pasach*, "to skip," "to pass by." In that dreadful night, possibly through an epidemic, Egypt's firstborn suffered the penalty the king himself should have paid for his obstinacy; innocent though they were, they were his subjects, his "creatures," and thus chained to his sin. The fatal blow that struck the Egyptians could not touch the Hebrews because the shielding wings of their Maker hovered over them. (Ex 12,13; cf. Is 31,5.) Forever, that night was to be the night of Israel's sparing, of the passing-by of cruel death.

THE MEANING OF THE UNLEAVENED BREADS   Tradition joined to the paschal feast another spring festival, originally separate from the first, that of the unleavened breads, *matsot*. It was a feast of farmers. While round about them nature put on new attire, they offered the first fruits of their barley harvest in gratitude and petition. (Lv 23,10.14) For seven days, nothing leavened was eaten; all fermented loaves were considered ritually unclean, for leaven was a sign of corruption, of evil influence. (Mt 16,5ff; 1 Cor 5,6–12) [3] No left-over dough was to contaminate the produce of the year-to-come, hence old leaven had to be cast out. A new start was needed; there would be a fresh sowing, another harvest, a young set of loaves.

To the Israelites of later generations, the expulsion of the old leaven, after a solemn search for it with a lighted candle throughout the house, was to be a reminder that in Egypt they had been infected with the delirium of idolatry, had been ill-thought of and ill-treated; that first they had been cheap laborers, despised by their masters, and then runaway slaves; that God had broken their chains; and that his infinite patience had shaped them into his people. Hence it is said of the month in which the reborn feast of the paschal lamb and the unleavened breads was to be celebrated in Israel: "This month shall stand at the head of your calendar; you shall reckon it the first month of the year." (Ex 12,2) What perfect symbols for the new life in Christ! St. Paul could thus demand of the community of Corinth, where an incestuous member had tried to make his father's wife his own, that they clear out every scrap of old leaven so that they might be like the Passover bread, new but unleavened. Since Christ, the paschal Lamb, was sacrificed for them, they were to keep life a feast, a feast, however, without the least trace of decaying leaven, indeed, one marked by "the unleavened bread of sincerity and truth." (1 Cor 5,7f)

When Israel joined the festival of the unleavened breads to that of the Passover, she transformed it completely. What was once an agricultural celebration became one of redemptive love. The anxiety over nature's unpredictableness was supplanted by confidence in God's fidelity; the bowing before the events of nature by praise of the events of salvific history. The tilling of the soil gave way to another kind of plowing and sowing: the inner renewal of the covenant of Yahweh.[4] "For seven days you shall eat with [the Passover sacrifice] only unleavened bread, the bread of affliction, that you may remember as long as you live the day of your departure from the land of Egypt; for in frightened haste you left the land of Egypt." (Dt 16,3) Once the two feasts—that of the unleavened breads and that of the meal of the lamb—were combined into one, they proved that, providentially, they had been designed for each other. They were a pair so interlocked that they illustrated the full meaning of the Exodus in a way one of them could never have done.

---

[3] For the opposite meaning of leaven as a sign of an upward movement, of the irrepressible expansion of God's reign, see Mt 13,33; Lk 13,21.

[4] This transformation was very much like that of a pagan festival into the nativity of our Lord. The early Church hallowed January sixth as his epiphany, his manifestation to the world. In the middle of the fourth century, however, the Latin Church began to celebrate the Lord's coming in the flesh on December twenty-fifth. For a long time, this day had been a feast of the Mithraic cult, held shortly after the winter solstice, when the day is shortest. From then on, the sun begins to assert itself; it is this "assertion" the Romans hailed on the twenty-fifth of December as *natalis invicti solis,* "the nativity of the unvanquished sun." The Church fathers had frequently called Christ the real or true Sun. The adaptation of the pagan feast was a prudent attempt to root out persisting remainders of paganism. It was also an appropriate move for it showed again that nature—so often man's enemy or, at least, a hindrance to things that are above it—reflects and is able to make vivid the mysteries of salvation.

FROM FAMILY FEAST TO NATIONAL HOLIDAY   At first, Passover was a liturgical event acted out within the family circle. It began at night for, as the Law hammered into the minds of the Israelites, it was *by night,* during the month of Abib (later called Nisan), that the Lord their God brought them out of Egypt. (Dt 16,1) On the first Passover, the ancient Hebrews kept a night of vigil for the Lord, and on that night he "stood guard" on their behalf. Thus all future generations were to keep watch with him. (Ex 12,42) All through Passover week, the Israelites lived in gratitude to God their Deliverer. (Ex 13,3–16; Dt 16,1–8) The seventh and final day was a day of solemnity and rest in honor of the Lord. (Dt 16,8) In the course of time, the family liturgy gave way to a Temple feast. (2 Chr 30; 35,1–19) No longer was the Passover, Israel's sparing, to be celebrated at one's home; whoever could, went to Jerusalem to fulfill the obligation of slaughtering the lamb in the Temple, God's chosen dwelling place, and to consume there the "roasted meat with unleavened bread and bitter herbs." (Ex 12,8) The vigil followed; in the morning, the watchers returned to their tents, which reminded them of the days when their ancestors had lived the unsettled life of nomads, indeed, united them to their forefathers' wanderings through the desert. (Dt 16,5ff) Such was the demand of the Law.

Once Passover had become a national holiday, some of its features changed. The lambs were still slaughtered in the Temple, but they were roasted on wooden spits in all the houses of Jerusalem. Four cups of wine were taken by each of the participants. Before the second, God was praised for having redeemed Israel from the sadness of Egypt so that she could be joyous in his service. At the time of the third, the participants remembered God who in his goodness gives bread to all flesh, who feeds and sustains all creatures. The partakers of the sacred meal did not drink the final cup without professing: "Though our mouth was full of song like the sea, though our tongue was shouting with joy like its raging billows . . . we should never thank you enough."

In those days, it was impossible for all the worshippers from afar— they may have varied from 80,000 to 120,000 or more—to find lodgings in the holy city with its 100,000 inhabitants. Many of the pilgrims lived, therefore, outside the city but ate the sacred meal within it, on rooftops or in courtyards. If an inhabitant of Jerusalem could open his home to a family that had come to join the community of Israel in its joy, he would gladly do so. Unfortunately, the national character of the feast sometimes had other than joyous effects. The large gatherings tempted the multitude to rebellion, to seditious riots against the presence of the "Roman eagle," its often harsh power and its idolatrous cult of the emperor. ·

74

THE SOLIDARITY OF GENERATIONS   The Deuteronomic precepts on the commemoration of the first Passover have one rare, extraordinary feature. They are put in the singular. They address each generation in Israel, and in each generation each member. When the Law says, "in frightened haste you left the land of Egypt" (Dt 16,3), each participant in the feast should know that he participates not only in the celebration of the moment but in God's mighty deeds of old. Indeed, the commemoration is more than a commemoration: The past is present, and the generation alive joins the generation in the wilderness. Each Israelite, then, was carried out of the land of bondage, led dry-shod through the sea, stood at Sinai, marched through the desert, and witnessed the covenant. Thus the *Haggadah*—the book containing the Seder, the order of ceremonies to be held at home on the first two nights of the festive week—declares:

> In every generation, each man is bound to look upon himself as if he himself had come forth from Egypt; as it is said: "On this day you shall explain to your son, 'This is because of what the Lord did for me when I came out of Egypt.'" (Ex 13,8) Our forefathers were not the only ones that the Holy One, blessed be he, redeemed; us, too, did he redeem along with them. . . .

Since the coming of Jesus, the interlocking of generations is no longer limited to the house of Jacob. Though the Sinaitic covenant was with the Jewish people only, all that happened during Israel's pilgrimage from the land of repression to that of promise—a pilgrimage that did not end with the crossing of the Jordan and the setting foot on the soil the Lord had assigned to the patriarchs (Gn 12,7; 26,3; 35,12; Ex 6,4)—was more than a phase of her national history. Her pilgrimage is an integral part of the spiritual history of mankind, for these were the days when the redemption of the world was prepared. Through the divine interventions of old, time was freed of that endless monotony of which the book Coheleth says: "What has been, that will be; what has been done, that will be done. Nothing is new under the sun." (Coh 1,9) Having been drawn into a mighty movement that now inched, then leaped, toward its appointed goal, the years of men lost their unhappy tedium.

Far from violating the principle that governs the Passover celebration, the bond between the old Israel and the new is its most wondrous application. In the New Dispensation, the sacred link that holds the descendants of Jacob together is expanded to envelop the earth, from end to end. Here, a new and greater intervention has joined the beginnings of salvific history to the fullness of time, the fullness of time to those beginnings, and both to the future manifestation of glory. If a Christian lives by faith, then, he is related to the men and women who trembled at Sinai; he is related, above all, to Mary and John who watched beneath the cross; to Mary of Magdala who rushed to the tomb which could not detain the risen Lord; to the eager company that awaited the wonder of Pentecost. By faith and worship, a Christian of any century is one with the first generation of Christ's followers, those witnesses who themselves heard, saw, and touched their

75

Master. In the communion of saints, the men and women of all generations, from Abraham to the end of time, are wayfarers together to the soil of the Lord, to the new Jerusalem. (Is 14,2; Ap 21,2)

At the Passover service, the reminder of the oneness of generations is followed by words of jubilation, words which in the course of centuries have been enlarged and embellished to read today:

> It is therefore upon us to thank, hymn, praise and acclaim, to exalt, honor, and bless, to glorify, extol, and adore him who wrought all these miracles for our fathers and for us. He led us out of the house of slavery into freedom, out of sorrow into joy, out of mourning into holiday, out of darkness into the great light, out of bondage into redemption. Let us therefore sing before him: Halleluia.

A Christian, saved in and through Christ, can hardly be less exuberant.

The worshipper's joy must be embodied, however, in his daily life, his praise proven and confirmed by concern for his fellows. Even if he were able to give homage to the Lord with the voice of angels but was, at the same time, devoid of love, he would sound no better than blaring brass. Even if he died a martyr's death but did not give himself wholly to the Lord, his sacrifice would leave him with nothing. (1 Cor 13,1ff) St. Paul's hymn extolling love as the heart of a life acceptable to God was prepared throughout the Old Testament, particularly by its prophets. Though the festive hour and day were set apart from the rest of the year, worship and life, the prophets insisted, were not to be divorced one from the other. In their eyes, ritual with no works of goodness to complement it was empty, indeed, abhorrent to Yahweh. Hands spread out in prayer were not to be employed in the use of dishonest weights or measures lest their pleading became blasphemy. Lips that uttered calumny could not be lips of thanksgiving; hearts closed to the need of neighbors were shut to God's grace, too. Hence Osea's challenge to the men of old as well as of today:

> Hear the word of the Lord. . . .
> Steadfast love I desire first, then sacrifice,[5]
> Knowledge of God more than holocausts.
> (Os 4,1; 6,6)

---

[5] In Hebrew, the above line reads: "Steadfast love (*chesed*) I desire, *not* sacrifice." As the following line (parallel to the first in meaning) shows, the "not" is dialectical—a device congenial, indeed, dear to biblical speech. By sharp contrast, by a seemingly unmitigated rejection, every dialectical negation is meant to bring out a truth human inertia tends to overlook. The truth Osea sought to burn into the minds of his hearers is that there is only one essential requirement: *chesed*, complete loyalty to the covenant. Without it, without knowledge of God—without obedience to, and union with, his will—offerings lose their value, sacrifices bear no fruit. Only as part of a total fidelity is man's worship pleasing to the Lord. (Cf. Am 5,21–24; Mi 6,6ff; Is 1,10–17; Jer 7,21ff; Ps 14[15].) Thus the verse in question is translated according to its intention, not its letter.

CHAPTER FIVE

PROMISE OF NEWNESS

At the Passover meal, Israel gloried in her birth as God's own people. Hence the Law rightly insisted: "No foreigner may partake of it." None but a member of the covenant had the right to be a companion of the festive joy. An alien dwelling in the holy land was to be admitted to the table only if, prior to the feast, he had been circumcised. (Ex 12,43–49) This exclusiveness was necessary for Israel's spiritual preservation but, to the prophetic vision, it was but a temporary restriction.

77

THE SIGNS OF NEWNESS

Isaia foresaw a day when the Lord of hosts would set a sumptuous table on Mount Sion for all the peoples of the earth.[1] It would be a day of jubilation, he predicted, a day when men would rejoice in God who will have answered their hope and saved them. (Is 25,6.9) Was the day to be near or far? In evaluating life around them and in foretelling the things-to-come, the prophets were interested, above all, in the plight of "today" as well as the judgment and hope of "tomorrow." As bearers of the word of God, their first task was to be molders of the future, the immediate future. But the word, whose witnesses they were, often ran ahead of them to undreamt horizons.

A NEW EXODUS   During the Babylonian exile, Israel's faith was upheld by the memory of the *tsedikot Yahweh,* the manifestations of God's faithfulness, his glorious deeds in rescuing her from Egyptian captivity. To the displaced, Isaia announced that, though their many infidelities had brought them to Babylon, the Lord's strong arm would lead them out again. "Fear not!" All who longed to return home, would return home. Feeble hands would be strengthened, and tottering knees made firm; blind eyes would be opened, and deaf ears cleared; the lame would leap like stags, and the mute sing. There would be no barren, no hostile desert to cross; streams and springs of water would welcome them instead.

> A highway will be there,
> called the holy way.
> (Is 35,8)

No weary march was to be ahead of them, rather a procession of triumphs. In rapture and delight, "crowned with everlasting joy" would the ransomed enter Sion. (Is 35) The everlasting joy that was to halo them and transfigure their beings suggested something greater than the return from temporary exile. Did it not point, beyond that return, to events of vast dimensions? Did it not point to a turn of history surpassing all those that went before?

The Second Isaia, too, made a new exodus his theme. In the spirit of the first, he had a voice cry out:

> In the desert prepare the way of the Lord!
> In the wasteland lay smooth a highway for our God!
> (Is 40,3)

God's visible presence, his glory, would be in the midst of the people, and together all mankind would see his radiance. Like a shepherd tending his flock, he would gather the lambs in his own arms. (Is 40,5.11) Though the prophet

---

[1] The Isaian vision forms the background of Jesus' saying that from the rising and the setting of the sun many will come to sup with Abraham, Isaac, and Jacob (Mt 8,11; Lk 13,28f), also of his parables of the royal wedding feast and the messianic banquet. (Mt 22,1–14; Lk 14,15–24)

promised that the barriers of Babylon would soon be lowered (Is 43,14), he seems to have looked farther than the things at hand. He seems to have looked at blessings of a distant future. As a matter of fact, he told his people in the name of Yahweh to forget the events of the past, to care no more for the happenings of long ago, for God was determined to do "a new thing": He would change the desert into a garden so that his people might drink and find refreshment. Thus says the Lord:

See, I am doing something new!
(Is 43,18ff)

Did St. Paul deceive himself when he saw these new wonders come true in Christ? If a man is "in Christ," that is, a disciple truly united with his Master, the apostle writes, he is a new creature: Oldness is gone, something new has sprung up. (2 Cor 5,17) No, the apostle was not mistaken. Christ was the answer to the prophetic cry for a holy newness and a new holiness—to the cry that was the impetus, the forward thrust of Israel's history. But St. Paul also knew that this thrust had not come to an end, that history continued to move— as it moves still—toward the second coming of Christ. For the moment, heaven receives, indeed, "retains" him, St. Peter told a multitude in Jerusalem, but when he returns, the "times of refreshment," "the times of the restoration of all things of which God has spoken by the mouth of his holy prophets," will have arrived, and the burning desire for newness will have found its ultimate fulfillment. (Ac 3,20f)

A NEW COVENANT   The prophetic hunger for "the new thing" God held in store for all flesh was felt and expressed in every possible way. The men of God knew that Israel had not always responded to the covenant as a people chosen, graced, and loved by the Lord should have, rather that she had often met his word with the mediocrity and fickleness that sit in the heart of every man. Worse than that, Osea had to accuse her of "harlotry," of running after contemptible lovers—the biblical metaphors for serving the gods of Chanaan, those personifications of fertility to whom the many unfaithful in Israel attributed the blessings of harvests. God's anger would come down on Israel like a storm but only to bring her back to him. He would "lead her into the desert," Osea announced, for a new betrothal, a new covenant, a covenant so rich that nature would be made a part of it. (Os 2,4–20) In the Israel of old, as in many other countries around the world even to this day, custom demanded that the bridegroom recompense the bride's family for losing her. The sum paid to the bride's father was more than a "bride-price"; it was a gift sealing the agreement. God's endowment sealing the new covenant promised by Osea would be gifts of another dimension: right and justice, love and mercy, fidelity and knowledge of the Lord. (Os 2,21f)

Jeremia, too, had to complain of Israel's sins. A people going from evil to evil; brother deceiving brother; violence, deceit, idolatry, stubbornness of heart covering the land—in Jeremia's eyes, these and other transgressions were so grave that he considered the covenant broken. (Jer 31,32)

79

Still, God was ready to start anew. The covenant he held out would be based on his forgiveness and its acknowledgment by the people. Henceforth, its members would do God's will in grateful awareness that they owed everything to his mercy. Anticipating St. Paul's teaching in his letter to the Romans, Jeremia foresaw that this experience of being children of mercy alone would become in them a fountain of knowledge, that is, of union with God. (Jer 31,34; Rom 5–6) Marked by a new economy, the covenant God was to grant would by far surpass the one given at Sinai. There, his voice thundered the commandments from the mountain but the people could not endure it. Fearful of his majestic presence, they remained at a distance, asking Moses to receive the Lord's message in their stead and bring it to them in his own words. (Ex 20,18–21)

Even though "God's own finger" had inscribed the commandments on tablets made of hardened earth (Dt 9,9), the tenfold "you shall not" was incapable of expressing God's innermost demand, incapable, too, of giving man the power to obey it. What Israel needed and what the Lord was happy to open to her was a new source of light, a new well of strength. She was to become a changed people: Her character was to be transformed and her heart renewed. Not on cold slabs of stone, then, but on a heart warm and alive would the Lord etch his *torah*, his teaching, his law: "I will make a new covenant with the house of Israel and the house of Juda. It will not be like the covenant I made with their fathers. . . . I will place my law within them and write it on their hearts." (Jer 31,31–34; cf. 32,38ff.)

The divine proclamation given through Jeremia clearly reveals the insufficiency but not the so-called formalism of the Old Law. Formalism was unknown to it except as an abuse. One has to say it again and again: the view that the Old Covenant demanded merely an outward show of compliance with the Law while the New alone requires the heart's obedience does justice neither to the spirit nor to the letter of the Ancient Dispensation. The legislative pages of Deuteronomy, for instance, are introduced by the imperative that Israel *seek* the Lord God with her whole heart and soul. They are governed by the great commandment that she *love* him with all her heart, soul, and strength. (Dt 4,29; 6,5)

The new heart—Ezechiel calls it a heart of flesh (Ez 36,26)—Jeremia envisions will be a spring of loving response. The prophet looks beyond the heart of the individual Israelite to a heart-to-come. He looks to a heart in Israel that will be the exemplar, the living model, the inspiration and the strength of hearts the world over. "Storehouse of divine bounty," the liturgy calls the heart of Jesus. It was opened by a lance so that from it streams of grace might pour out upon men everywhere. (Preface to the feast of the Sacred Heart)

A NEW DAVID, A NEW TEMPLE   There was no end to the longing for newness. Disappointed by her many kings—caricatures rather than real servants of God and of the people—Israel yearned for a return of the days of David. Every descendant and successor of the great king enkindled in her new hope; almost every one quenched it again. In foretelling the advent of the good ruler, the prophets spoke in a single breath of God the Lord and David his servant. Both were to be sought together, both to shepherd Israel in perfect unison. (Os 3,5; Ez 34,23f) Indeed, a prince of peace would sit on David's throne forever. (Is 9,5f)

> A shoot shall sprout from the stump of Jesse,
> and from his roots a bud shall blossom.
> The spirit of the Lord shall rest upon him. . . .
> (Is 11,1f)

"Shoot" was a term for the promised King-Messia, who did not come till the birth of Jesus. Hence, in introducing him to the world, the New Testament writers stress that he is the offspring of David. (Mt 1,1; Lk 1,32; Rom 1,3; Ap 5,5) Each synoptic evangelist tells the story of the man (in one case, two men) who, outwardly blind but having eyes of faith, was bold enough to beg the return of his sight. In a cry that shattered the air, he became the mouthpiece of the weary and burdened everywhere: "Son of David, have mercy on me!" (Mk 10,47f; Mt 20,30f; Lk 18,38f)

In describing a new Sion, the prophet became poet. "Storm-battered and unconsoled," Jerusalem would be rebuilt. Her foundations, pavements, and pinnacles, her walls and her gates would be made of sapphires, emeralds, rubies, carbuncles, and other precious stones. The jewels were symbolic of the reign-to-come: the reign of truth, of justice, and of peace. (Is 54,11–15; cf. Ap 21,9–21.) The transformed Sion would be for men from everywhere: Her walls would be called "salvation," her gates "praise." (Is 60,3.6.18) Among the utterances of Zacharia is one that points to a man called Shoot who would rebuild the Temple and rule as king. (Za 6,12f) The Temple was indeed restored. When the true Shoot, long-awaited Son and Lord of David, arrived, he answered those in Israel who challenged his authority by pointing to his body: "Destroy this temple, and in three days I will raise it up." (Jn 2,19) With these words, he announced the sacrificial, and thus blessed, slaying of his body as well as its rising as the new sanctuary. On another occasion, he could say that "here"—in his own person—there was something "greater than the temple." (Mt 12,6)

THE NEW PASCHAL MEAL

Exile, its grief, and other sorrows that beset the ancient Israel were not the principal causes of the prophetic cry for a renewal of all things. Israel's distress acted very much like hostile bacteria invading a healthy body. The body rallies to its own defense; more than that, its healing power and regenerative capacity are set in motion to restore its strength. The comparison, however, is far from perfect. Israel's life often went from sickness to health, and to sickness again. At her beginning, however, stands God's summons; she was a communal body called into existence by grace. Hence, the *élan* implanted in her worked toward something greater than mere restoration. Her sins could not prevent her history—which at all times was, whether she realized it or not, the history of man's salvation—from being alive with hope. And this was God's doing.

THE UNIVERSAL PASCH   Despite the scorn and death threats to which Jeremia was exposed, he was the happy bearer of this good news:

> Behold, I will bring [the remnant of Israel] back
>   from the land of the north;
> I will gather them from the ends of the world,
>   with the blind and the lame in their midst. . . .
>   (Jer 31,8)

It must have been around 587 B.C., the year of Jerusalem's destruction and the deportation of its leading citizens into captivity, that these words were spoken. About 300 years later, or more, when the Jews of Alexandria had the Hebrew Scriptures put into Greek—the so-called Septuagint—the translator of Jeremia rendered the final verse differently. In a kind of "rereading," as exegetes call it—that is, in an interpretative translation guided by a clearer insight into God's design—he wrote:

> I will gather them from the ends of the earth
>   for the feast of the Passover.
>   (Jer 38,8) 2

The truest in Israel, her holy remnant, eagerly awaited this new, universal, and lasting Pasch. Unwittingly, under the guise of strange, often weird, ceremonies, even pagans may have yearned for this meal of meals. When "on the day before he suffered" (canon of the Mass), Jesus entered the upper room and sat down with his companions of three years for his last Passover, he gave voice to this mighty expectation in words most intimate. Rarely did he grant to those around him a glimpse of his inner life. At that moment, he did. He told them that he had longed, with all the intensity of his heart, to eat this Passover with them before undergoing his passion. He also assured them that he would not eat it again till its meaning had attained complete fulfillment in the kingdom of God. (Lk 22,15f) Thus, the last supper with the small band of his apostles was the anticipation of the future meal of millions, the advance enactment of the great banquet of messianic times. (Is 25,6) Indeed, at that hour the final period of history—whatever its duration may be—had begun.

THE LAST SUPPER: PROBLEM AND SOLUTIONS   Several scholars have doubted that the Lord's parting supper was a Passover meal. Their doubt stems

---

2 The chapter divisions of the Hebrew and Greek versions of the book of Jeremia are not identical throughout.

from one of the most difficult exegetical problems with which Scripture confronts us. According to the unanimous testimony of the synoptics, Jesus celebrated the last supper as a paschal meal on the eve of the Passover, "on the first day of the Unleavened Bread." (Mt 26,17; Mk 14,12; Lk 22,7) But according to St. John, it was on the eve of the feast, on "the Preparation Day for the Passover, about the sixth hour" (Jn 19,14) that Pilate handed Jesus over to the soldiers to be crucified. At first sight, these two statements seem contradictory, hence a biblical scholar has the task of reconciling them. Should he fail—perhaps because a small item of life or worship in Jesus' day has been irretrievably lost to us—and thus be forced to confess: "I do not know," his lack of knowledge would not disgrace him. Faith has been given to the believer and wisdom to the theologian, not in order to know every detail of sacred history but rather to love God and the things that come from and lead to him.

Without the least biblical support, some writers have seen in the last supper a religious meal of the kind the so-called *chaburot* were wont to hold. *Chaburot*, "companies," were societies of men devoted to the keeping of the Law. We know of pharisaic fraternities whose purpose was to observe the regulations regarding clean and unclean food in the strictest possible manner. Quite apart from the fact that every Jewish meal was a religious one—even to have the meager breakfast of bread, salt, and water without giving thanks to God would have been unthinkable—the fellowship of the apostles with their Master was not a *chaburah* pledged to a life of ritual purity. Its calling and intent were quite different. In any case, there is no biblical support for this theory.

Another theory considers St. John's language symbolic rather than historical. Those who hold it suggest that, in "antedating" the passion by one day, the evangelist wanted to proclaim, by a symbol as it were, that Jesus was the true paschal Lamb. For the ninth hour, the hour of his death on Golgotha, was about the time when, in the Temple not far away, the paschal lambs of the old Passover were slain. That their slaughter prefigured his death, and that his death fulfilled theirs, is unquestionably St. John's view, as it has been the belief of the whole Church through the centuries. But to have recourse to a "symbolic" interpretation of the Johannine date would seem too easy a solution.

There have been other serious attempts to harmonize the two seemingly opposite statements: the synoptic one that Jesus supped with his apostles on what we understand to be the 14th of Nisan and was nailed to the cross on the next day, and the Johannine one that the Lord was crucified on the 14th of that month. A contemporary Catholic scholar, Mlle. Annie Jaubert, holds that in New Testament times two calendars were in existence: a more recent lunar one, used by official Judaism, and an ancient solar one, used among others by the monks of Qumrân. To follow the first, the phases of the moon had to be observed since the Passover was to be celebrated at the first full moon after the spring equinox. (Significantly, one of the names given to calendar science by Jewish tradition is "sanctification of the moon.") The other calendar, however, had feasts so stabilized that the 14th of Nisan—the eve of the Passover—always fell on a Tuesday. Mlle. Jaubert suggests that, like the community of Qumrân, Jesus followed the supposedly ancient reckoning. If he actually did, he would have died on the 14th of Nisan according to the official, priestly calendar (that is, on Friday of Holy Week) but would have held the last supper on the 14th of

83

Nisan according to what seems to have been a sectarian counting of the days and months of the year (that is, on the Tuesday of Holy Week).

This hypothesis is ingenious but it creates as many difficulties as it seems to solve. The last supper, for instance, could not have been a true Passover meal since it would have been held without a paschal lamb. It seems dubious, too, that Jesus would have wanted to celebrate the Passover in the manner of Qumrân and by this gesture associate himself with the monks who—for all their earnestness and devotion—were rebels against the Temple priesthood, schismatics who wanted no traffic with either Jewish officialdom or anyone not of their ranks. Jesus was no rebel or separatist. No matter how severely he castigated the people and its leaders, he would not shatter his enduring bond with them. Living and dying in their midst, he, the Lord, was one of them.

An interesting explanation was offered by the late Père Lagrange. To understand it, one needs to remember that Jews did not begin the day at midnight but at sunset. Nevertheless, they counted the days as we do. For them, the evening of the 14th of Nisan was really part of the next day; still, it was called the evening of the 14th. Hence it could be said that the paschal meal took place on the 14th, though the 15th was really the feast of the Unleavened Bread. The Law required that the lamb be "slaughtered during the evening twilight." (Ex 12,6) The Sadducees, on the one hand, taught that the hours between six and half-past seven in the evening were the only lawful ones for the slaying. The Pharisees, on the other, permitted the sacrifice as early as half-past three, even an hour earlier if it had to be performed on the eve of the Sabbath.

By their rigidity, the Sadducees were caught in a dilemma. What was to be done when the 15th of Nisan fell on a Sabbath, the day of complete repose? Since the Sabbath, like every other day, began the evening before, the lambs could certainly not be immolated close to sunset. The question was whether the Sabbath obligation to refrain from all work should yield to the requirements of the Passover. Most Pharisees answered in the affirmative and thus avoided the entanglement. The Sadducean answer was "No." They held fast to both principles, that of strict observance of the Sabbath rest and that of the sacrifice of the Passover lamb at dusk.

The only way out of the predicament was for the Sadducees to allow the slaughter of the animals a day ahead of time. This would not have altered the date of the feast and would have kept the sanctity of the Sabbath intact. The Sadducees ordered, therefore, an earlier slaughter but did not eat the lamb till the evening of the next day. There were others, however, who thought that once immolated, the lamb should be consumed on the same evening, although they had to hold the paschal meal a day before the true beginning of the feast. Since, in the year of Jesus' death, the 15th of Nisan happened to be a Sabbath, the problem became acute. It might well have been, Père Lagrange muses, that the apostles—with the exception of Judas, all Galileans, countryfolk attached to old customs—favored the practice of eating the lamb the day of its sacrifice. Hence they were in no way astonished when their Master, like many other pilgrims, celebrated the Pasch with them a day earlier than the Temple rulers thought correct. (M.-J. Lagrange, O.P., *The Gospel of Jesus Christ* [London: Burns Oates & Washbourne, 1938], II, 193f.)

Some forty years ago, the German scholar Paul Billerbeck offered still an-

84

other solution which Canon Ricciotti, among others, adopted almost entirely. In our day, the calendar is fixed by common consent and changed only by international agreement. In the days of the Israel of old, the dates for the major feasts were determined mainly by the direct but not always easy observation of the new moon. The final determination was in the hands of a Sanhedrin commission for calendar affairs which went about its work empirically and often with a certain flexibility. Billerbeck assumes that in the year of Christ's passion the commission, largely under Sadducean control, had the beginning of the month of Nisan fixed in such a way that the first day of Passover fell on a Sabbath. Automatically, the Feast of Weeks or Pentecost occurred seven weeks later, on the day after the Sabbath.[3] Pharisees and Sadducees were then engaged in a bitter struggle for the decisive voice in religious matters. The unyielding Pharisees threatened with counter measures unless the calendar was so regulated as to have the 15th of Nisan come on a Friday, and Pentecost therefore on a Saturday. Fearful of their opponents' influence on the people, the Sadducees consented to a compromise. They gave permission to the Pharisees to celebrate Passover on Thursday whereas they themselves clung to Friday.

This split between the two major powers in Israel compelled Jesus to choose between one date or the other. Being a man pursued, yet filled with the urgency of his mission—in biblical language, knowing that his appointed hour was near (Mt 26,18)—he decided to eat the paschal meal at the same time as the majority of the people would, following the pharisaic example. Thus the synoptics were right when, with the people's practice in mind, they called the day of the last supper "the first day of the Unleavened Bread" or "the day of the Unleavened Bread, on which the paschal lamb had to be slaughtered." (Mt 26,17; Mk 14,12; Lk 22,7) St. John, too, was correct in making use of the official date and calling Good Friday "the Preparation Day for the Passover" (Jn 19,14), that is, the day of immolation of the Passover victims. This fact gave him an opportunity to bring out more forcefully that Christ was the perfect Lamb, the Lamb of God taking away the sin of the world. (Jn 1,29) (Strack-Billerbeck, *Kommentar zum Neuen Testament aus Talmud und Midrasch* [Munich: C. H. Beck, 1924], II, 851ff; cf. Giuseppe Ricciotti, *The Life of Christ* [Milwaukee: Bruce, 1947], pp. 566ff.)

Despite outward disagreement, then, the synoptics and St. John are in accord. The conflict of dates in their accounts was not of their own making; it only mirrored a conflict within their own people. Even if we lacked any convincing hypothesis for settling the discrepancy, several details related by the evangelists without particular stress, almost casually, point unmistakably to a paschal meal. According to their explicit testimony, the apostles asked their Master's wish for the Passover. Immediately, he sent two of them to prepare all that was needed for its celebration. Following his directions, they found a large upstairs room, all furnished and ready, no doubt in the house of one of Christ's friends or disciples. (Mt 26,17ff; Mk 14,12–15; Lk 22,7–13)

The week before, Jesus had been in Bethany. Had he simply wished to celebrate a "friendship-meal," he could have returned there. But he remained

---

[3] The Feast of Seven Weeks or Pentecost, a thanksgiving festival, received its name from its date. It was held seven weeks or fifty days after the Sabbath of Passover week. (Lv 23,15f; Ex 34, 22; Dt 16,10) Later tradition attached to it the commemoration of the proclaiming of the commandments on Mount Sinai.

85

in crowded Jerusalem, for tradition prescribed that the paschal lamb be eaten within the gates of the holy city. The common people usually ate in their courtyards or kitchens; only the rich had dining rooms in the Graeco-Roman manner. Every Passover, however, was a special occasion, and this one a most special event. While the habitual mealtimes were in the morning and late afternoon or early evening—before and after work—Jesus held his last supper late in the evening. (Mk 14,17; Mt 26,20) It lasted, as no ordinary meal would have, well into the night. (Jn 13,30; 1 Cor 11,23)

After Jesus and the twelve entered the festively lighted room, they reclined on pillows placed in a U-shaped curve around a low oval or rectangular table, each resting on his left hand in order to keep the right one free. (Jn 13,12.23) Of foreign origin, a leaning posture on a carpet, cushion, or couch was contrary to native practice. At the paschal meal, however, this posture was a duty: It was a symbol of liberty by which even the poorest man in Israel proved that, thanks to God's intervention in the days of old, he was born in freedom. Again, though the disciples were dismayed by their Master's grim prediction that one of them would betray him (Mt 26,21f), they seem to have been completely undisturbed by Judas's early departure. The only meaningful explanation of their calm is the paschal custom of inviting the hungry to share in the meal or of assisting them in some other way. The apostles must have assumed that Judas, keeper of the purse, had gone out in order to distribute alms among the beggars that always lingered in the Temple area. Finally, two evangelists mention almost in passing that the supper ended with the singing of a hymn (Mt 26,30; Mk 14,26) which was, no doubt, the second part of the Hallel. (Pss 113B–117[115–118]) These psalms conclude, even to this day, the essential parts of the Passover service.

THE UNFOLDING OF THE LAST SUPPER   To state that the last supper was a Passover meal—and the author of this book does so emphatically— is not to say that Jesus was a slave to its ordinances. Master even of the Sabbath (Mt 12,8; Mk 2,28; Lk 6,5)—Israel's delight (Is 58,13), God's gift bestowing blessings of a kind toil can never yield (Prv 10,22)—he was no less Sovereign over the paschal rites. Indeed, there was something unique about him, at all times. The disciples at Emmaus, blinded by grief, did not recognize him till he took the bread, blessed, broke and handed it to them. (Lk 24,30f) It was hardly his outward manner of taking, breaking, and distributing the bread—the very mechanics of his acts—that differed from the ways of other men. What stood out must have been a gesture of singular love or a thanksgiving that did not follow an acknowledged usage, however venerable, but was Christ's intimate prayer, opening to his hearers new vistas of God's world.

The Passover service began in Jesus' time, as it does today, with the chanting of the *kiddush*, the "sanctification" of the first of the four cups of wine ordained for the Seder: "Blessed are you, O Lord our God, King of the universe, Creator of the fruit of the vine." With these or other words, Jesus, too, gave thanks and then added: "Take this and share it among you; for I say to you that I will not drink of the fruit of the vine, until the king-

86

dom of God comes." (Lk 22,17f) Thus, at the beginning of the supper, Jesus announced that the old Pasch was to be superseded by a new one.

After the first cup of sparkling red wine had made its round among the company, pitcher, basin, and towel were offered to the master of the Seder so that he might wash his hands. In all likelihood, it was at this moment that Christ took off his upper garment, fastened a towel around his waist, poured water into the basin and, like a servant, washed the apostles' feet. He was, indeed, their Servant—everyone's Servant—leading them to a new life in which, rather than lording over others as man's imperious instinct demands, they would be co-workers of joy. (2 Cor 1,23) St. John is the only evangelist to tell the story of the footwashing. (Jn 13,4–20) He introduces it and other narratives related to the last supper—remaining silent about its substance because he gave attention to its mystery earlier in his gospel (Jn 6)—with a stirring comment. Christ loved his own while he was with them, the evangelist marvels; about to be separated from them, he loved them to the utmost and to the last. (Jn 13,1)

After the washing of feet, some herbs were probably brought in: raw vegetables like lettuce, radishes, celery, endive, parsley, or cress. It was the custom for the master of the Seder to dip them in salt water or vinegar and hand a piece to each one present. They served as hors d'oeuvres. Later, at the meal proper, they were eaten again, this time dipped in a special sauce, called *charoset,* made of crushed almonds, figs, dates, and vinegar. The eating of bitter herbs was to keep alive the memory that the stay in Egypt—for which, in moments of discouragement or despair, the wanderers in the desert had longed (Ex 16,3; Nm 14,2)—was filled with bitterness. The ritual required the head of the family to break one of the flat cakes of unleavened bread in two. Wrapping one half in a cloth, he put it aside; named the *afikoman,* it was to be eaten as a dessert or afterdish. Those near the master lifted up the platter on which the other part of the cake rested, while all the diners recited: "This is the bread of poverty our forefathers ate in the land of Egypt. Come and eat, all who hunger! Come to the Passover, all who are in need!"

Was it then that Jesus spoke his words of newness, of the new Pasch, the new sacrifice, the new presence: "This is my body which will be delivered up for you"? (Lk 22,19) Did the new saying take the place of the revered one repeated by generation after generation? Or did Jesus let the old meal run its course and then crown it with the new? There are arguments in favor of both possibilities but even the most cautious choice might best be postponed till the entire paschal meal has been described.

A second cup of wine was taken. Its enjoyment, as much as the other actions related so far, was only an overture to the real supper. During its solemnities (today prior to them), the one who presided over the meal was duty-bound to enlarge upon Israel's first creed. (Dt 26,5–9) The only rabbinic directive given for this homily is that "it begin with shame and end with praise." "Shame" obviously refers to the admission that the Hebrews in Egypt were idolators and slaves, while "praise" bespeaks God's work in setting them free. From shame to praise, from humiliation to glory is a summing up of sacred history, yet it is also a testimonial, however unintended, to the life of Christ. After another washing of hands—this time by the whole company—another breaking of unleavened bread, ordinarily made of wheat, and another taste of the bitter herbs described before, the paschal lamb was brought in: It had been roasted over an open fire and was to be served whole. Having been blessed, it was artfully cut and everyone given his share.

As the supper drew to its close, the up-to-now hidden *afikoman* was distributed among the table companions and the third cup was filled but not touched till God had been given his due. The master of the house asked that a blessing be said. "Let us bless him, our God, of whose food we have eaten," to which the participants added: "and through his goodness we live." Among the words of the prayer was this praise:

> Through his great goodness, food has never failed us,
>   and may it never fail us, for his great Name's sake.
> For he feeds and sustains all, and does good unto all,
>   and prepares food for all his creatures which he created.
> Blessed are you, O Lord, who feeds all.

After this thanksgiving, which brought the meal proper to its conclusion, a fourth cup was poured and the second part of the Hallel sung. (Ps 113B–117[115–118]) The singing ended with the repetition of a number of verses, among which were these:

> Pray Lord, save us. . . .
> Blessed is he who comes in the name of the Lord.
>   (Ps 117[118]25f)

Without pretending to read Jesus' mind, might one not assume the following order? In his divine generosity but no less out of reverence for the Law—true Son, indeed truest Son of Israel that he was—he wanted first the old banquet to unfold itself in all its beauty so that, at its climax, he could fulfill and transform it. The signs, elements, and gestures remained the same, the words and the meaning were new. Very likely, then, Jesus used for the institution of the eucharist (the Greek translation of *berachah,* "blessing," "thanksgiving") the *afikoman,* the bread that had been concealed through the main part of the service, and the third cup of wine, called "the cup of blessing." (1 Cor 10,16)

THE SIGNIFICANCE OF THE LAST SUPPER   Whatever interpretation one accepts—be it the one that sees the words of institution enveloping the old Pasch or the other that sees in them its breathtaking conclusion—the event itself is incontestable. Of the four accounts we possess, the oldest

88

is that of St. Paul in his first letter to the Corinthians, written about 56 A.D.[4] There he speaks of a teaching he "received from the Lord." It was obviously much earlier that he learned of the events of Holy Thursday through his co-apostles in Jerusalem and through the churches whose life he shared, particularly that of Antioch. Both the apostles and the communities into which St. Paul was received were Christ's instruments. From the outset, the new Pasch was part of the apostolic preaching; and from the earliest days of the Church, the eucharist was the core of her prayer everywhere. St. Paul's emphatic "from the Lord" identifies Christ as the origin of her doctrine and worship; it testifies to the purity of her tradition, indeed, to the union between Christ and the community of his faithful.

Rather than reproduce St. Paul's account, it might be more rewarding to offer a composite drawn from all four sources, not unlike the one the Church uses for the act of consecration in the Latin rite:

> The night Jesus was handed over [to the authorities who plotted his death], while he supped [with his disciples], he took the bread, pronounced the blessing, broke it, and gave it [to them] with these words: "Take, eat! This is my body which shall be given up for you. Do this in memory of me." In like manner, after he had supped, he took the cup, offered thanks, and gave it to them with these words: "Drink, all of you! This is the cup of the new covenant in my blood which shall be shed for you and many, unto the forgiveness of sins. As often as you drink of it, do it in memory of me."

If one listens to the original tone of the words of institution, they have a freshness and vigor our familiarity with them tends to spoil. First, "This is my body" sounds much stronger in Aramaic, Christ's own tongue. In it, the saying is an unadorned "This my body" or, as many exegetes assume, "This my flesh"—flesh being the common idiom for living body. (Cf. Jn 6,52.54–58.) Here the "is" is missing, for neither Hebrew nor Aramaic, neither the sacred nor the popular language of Jesus' day, expressed the copula. The bare juxtaposition of "this" and "my flesh," with its resulting simplicity, immediately suggests the identity between the food in the hands

---

[4] The fact of four different accounts (Mt 26,26ff; Mk 14,22ff; Lk 22,19f; 1 Cor 11,23ff)—the first two and the last two akin to one other but none varying from the other substantially—confirms their authenticity. Were they the same to the last syllable, there could be no doubt of their being a construct. Did they contradict each other, they could hardly be relied on. In their accidental variance but substantial identity, however, they are a witness to the historicity of the event and the veracity of its narrators. In their accounts, we hear the true voice of the Lord, as understood by the sacred writers and as reflected in the liturgies of which they were leaders or participants. To give but one instance, "This cup is the new covenant in my blood" (1 Cor 11,25; Lk 22,20) and "This is the blood of the new covenant" (Mt 26,27; Mk 14,24) assert the same reality, though the first saying must have appeared less harsh to Jewish ears because of the use of metonymy, that figure of speech which substitutes one word for another it suggests, in this instance the container—"cup"—for the thing contained—"blood."

of the Speaker and the Speaker himself. The same holds true of Christ's words over the cup. Second, both sayings begin with a mere "this," and not with "this bread" or "this cup." What Christ thus gave to his followers was not mere symbols but his body to eat and his blood to drink; so the Church has always understood his words. In the old Passover ritual, the master of the house explains the significance of the meal's elements and actions; his words of interpretation form an important part of the service. The Master of the new Passover rite, however, *does* things. His words have all the characteristics of divine words: They do more than interpret, they "create," they convert, they effect what they signify, they accomplish what they set out to do.

Third, shining through the significative meaning of Jesus' utterances over bread and wine is another, wider one. We, too, speak of counting "heads" when inquiring after the number of persons in a given place or we call the inhabitants of a town "souls." The disposition of mind that sees totalities though only parts are mentioned is much stronger in the Semitic languages. "Body" ("flesh") and "blood" are thus to the ancient Hebrews more than terms of anatomy or physiology. In addition to their significative meaning, they have a more comprehensive, indeed, a total one. "Body" ("flesh") is also the entire man as the senses perceive him, while blood, the pulsating source of life, points to his whole existence. Ultimately, then, "my body (flesh)" implies "I, the One you see and hear"; "my blood," implies "I who am in your midst, loving you." [5] Fourth, as "body" ("flesh") and "blood" spell life, so do they spell death. They are man in his mortality. Hence when speaking of his body and his blood—body to be surrendered, blood to be shed—Jesus uses sacrificial language. His body is that of the Servant smitten and pierced, of "the Lamb led to the slaughter" (Is 53,4.7), and his blood that of the perfect Victim, shed to atone, save, and seal a new covenant. (Ex 24,4–8; Is 49,6) Fifth, this blood is shed for "many"—another Hebrew and Aramaic idiom. "Many" is neither the opposite of "a few" nor that of "all." Rather does it bespeak an unseen multitude, imposing no restriction or limits on their number. It proclaims the

---

[5] Tradition has never wavered in its proclamation of Christ's total presence in the eucharist. The Council of Trent, in particular, made this mystery part of defined doctrine. Faced in its day with a novel teaching that denied the sacrificial character of the eucharist and made Christ's presence dependent on the faith of the recipient, the Council, following St. Thomas (*S.Th.*, 3ᵃ,76,1ff), not only distinguished between the direct and indirect effects of Christ's words, but stressed this distinction. The transfigured body of the risen Lord is present under the veil of bread, his glorious blood under the veil of wine *vi verborum,* the Council declared, that is, through the immediate power of the words. Blood and soul, however, are present under the species of bread, body and soul under the species of wine, *vi naturalis connexionis et concomitantiae,* that is, by virtue of their organic unity, their companionship and coexistence. The Lord's divinity, too, is present in the holy eucharist under both appearances, since the hypostatic union, the oneness of the two natures in the divine Person of Christ, links it forever to his humanity. (D876[1639]; *TCT*721) While the linguistic analysis elucidates the Church's teaching, her *magisterium* confirms the exegete's findings.

universality of the New Covenant; for the "many" are the billions of all times and all places to be justified. (Is 53,11)

The words with which Jesus instituted the new Pasch reveal him as Priest and Gift, as High Priest forever, as the Gift of perfect worship to the Father, and as the Gift of salvation nourishing his own. His words anticipated his passion and, at the same time, pointed beyond it. When he entered the places of his condemnation and mounted the hill of his execution, he did so with the sureness of victory. He knew that his "appointed way" would make him pass through suffering and death—unharmed. Though the Firstborn who is before all creation (Col 1,15), he was not spared the agony of the dying, and deep into his side did the soldier thrust his spear in order to prove that he was "gone." Yet, he ascended from the tomb, in a body no longer mortal but flooded, indeed, flowing over with the power of the Spirit. "The Son of Man is to be betrayed into the hands of men, and they will kill him; and on the third day he will rise again." (Mt 17,21f)

THE FRUIT OF THE LAST SUPPER   Among the several psalms Christ and his disciples recited before leaving the upper room for the Mount of Olives, was one that held a prominent place in the Temple liturgy as a processional and hymn of thanksgiving. Tradition seems to have demanded that it be sung antiphonally, by leader and congregation alternating with one another. It is not at all improbable that the little group gathered around Jesus did likewise. If this was the case, then he, the Head of the meal community, recited these verses among others, giving them for the first time their full significance:

> I shall not die, but live
>   and declare the works of the Lord.
>   (Ps 117[118]17)

And his companions answered:

> The stone which the builders rejected
>   has become the cornerstone.
> By the Lord has this been done;
>   it is wonderful in our eyes.
> This is the day the Lord has made;
>   let us be glad and rejoice in it.
>   (Ps 117[118]22ff)

Despite this comfort, there was little rejoicing among the apostles. That night their hearts were heavy, not yet warmed by the fire of Pentecost. They could not have grasped the full meaning of what had happened in their presence: that their Lord, though himself a Guest in another man's house, was Host not only to them but to the whole world. There, in the upper room, the leading themes of the Ancient Dispensation—word, witness, deliverance, revelation, covenant, expiation, sacrifice, sacrament, and

91

the reign of God—converged. Christ was at one and the same time Sacrificer and Sacrifice. Past and future were drawn into that moment, and into every moment in which henceforth Christ's command would be obeyed, his words and actions repeated, his saving deeds sacramentally commemorated. On the one hand, Israel's many sacrificial meals were fulfilled, particularly the one solemnizing the covenant at Sinai. (Ex 24,11) On the other, Isaia's final banquet "of rich food and fine wines" for all mankind (Is 25,6)—that is, mankind's happy gathering around the living God, manifest in the Christ of glory—was anticipated. It continues to be anticipated wherever Mass is celebrated, hence the assurance: "As often as you eat this bread and drink the cup, you proclaim the Lord, *until he comes.*" (1 Cor 11,26)

This proclamation is not by words alone. Christ's bidding: "Do this in memory of me," means that the new Pasch like the old is a *zikkaron*, a memorial, an objective recollection under the signs of the sacrament, a remembrance not merely in thought but also in deed. As the diners at the Passover, by their participation in the meal, became part of the generation the Lord himself had redeemed from servitude, so do the partakers of the eucharist become Christ's "contemporaries." Though their eyes do not see him, the encounter with him is real and immediate. At Mass, Christ's work of redemption is made present for our sake so that on Holy Thursday the Church can say of him that "the day before he suffered for our salvation and the salvation of all men, that is, *today,* he took bread into his holy and worshipful hands. . . ."

Every day is such a "today." It is this immediacy that bestows on Christians what St. Paul calls *koinōnía*, "communion," "fellowship," "sharing": a sharing of the blood of Christ and a partaking of his body. (1 Cor 10,16) Hence, the Christian is lifted into communion with the whole Christ, Christ crucified and risen, human and divine, Christ the Head and his members. Christ, the new Pasch, binds the Christian even to the triune God, and to his brethren as well. "We, the many, are one body in Christ," needing and serving one another as do the members of a body. (Rom 12,5) The Lord's table is the warrant of the Church's unity. From there the community is continuously rebuilt, renewed; from there the individual Christian is ever refreshed and refashioned. The "one bread" begets that fellowship, that participation in the spirit which is the source of harmony and warm affection (Phil 2,1); it is the seed of everlasting life (Jn 6,54–59), the medicine of immortality, and the antidote against death. (Ignatius of Antioch, *To the Ephesians,* 2,20)

CHAPTER SIX

DEATH, RESURRECTION, THE DAY OF YAHWEH

For many generations, Jacob's descendants—in biblical language the "sons of Israel"—dwelt in the northeastern part of the Nile delta, first as a tribe of shepherds, afterward as forced laborers. On their arrival, they were welcomed by the then ruler of Egypt, later they were oppressed by another who considered their fruitfulness a threat to his power. Without qualm, he ordered their newborn sons killed, while he had the fathers driven to work on the construction of two cities designed to assure his strategy of trade, war, and conquest. Strangely, neither in the days of their freedom nor in the time of their enslavement did the Israelites accept the Egyptian dream of the fields of paradise that supposedly awaited man after his death.

The picture the Egyptians painted of man's afterlife was not of a piece. Still, the sun's "movements" seem to have been the foundation of their thought: As the sun-god "died" every night but "rose again" the next morning, so the dead awakened in another world to happiness, provided their journey had been a safe one. There were all kinds of dangers: from serpents or foul waters, for instance. The eastern horizon was the approach to "heaven"; none could pass, none enter who was not aware, among other things, of the secret names of the door, its parts and its keeper, who could not recite flawlessly the necessary spells and magic formulae, who did not know how to utter protestations of guiltlessness and thus prevail upon his judges. The next world was not unlike the present one; in fact, it was a continuation or, rather, an improved version of life on earth. There as here, men ate and drank, plowed, reaped, and threshed, fought and loved. There was one marked difference, however. The realm of the dead was one of comfort; misery was banished from the fields of peace; everyone expected to be a lord, and no longer a serf.

These reveries, one would think, should have appealed to the Israelites as much as they impressed the Egyptians. Indeed, they should have been doubly attractive to men who were treated like prisoners of war. Their oppressor had succeeded in breaking their spirit. Under his rod, they had become slaves in mind as well as in fact: frightened, submissive to all the little despots he had set over them but inveighing against Moses, their own brother and liberator. (Ex 2,14; 5,21) Nonetheless, the Egyptian concept of a fairy-tale heaven left them unimpressed. As they departed from the region of Goshen in the northeastern corner of Egypt, and for centuries after, they still clung to the sober, indeed, depressing views Abraham had absorbed in his ancestral land or, at least, to ideas that strikingly resembled those of Babylonia. For the Babylonians, the abode of the dead was a dismal place no one could penetrate, a land from which there was no return—a house of darkness.

LIFE AFTER DEATH

When one realizes how strongly Israel's faith contrasted with that of her environment, in fact opposed it, her seeming inability to free herself from the dreary views of Babylonia poses a psychological as well as a theological problem that vexes the mind.

94

THE ENIGMATIC STANDSTILL OF FAITH   There must have been powerful reasons why for many centuries Israel, the people of hope, remained the captive of Babylonian hopelessness. *Asirey ha-tikvah,* "prisoners of hope," is one of the prophetic designations for the men of the covenant. (Za 9,12) Even in the hour of exile and oppression, they remained hopeful, indeed, were chained to hope. But for a long time their hope bore chains as well. It was centered in God as the Lord of history who governed and guarded the people's destiny, who showed favor and love to the individual Israelite during his days on earth but— so Israel believed for over a millennium—almost none in the life-to-come.

There must have been other than natural reasons for the chosen people to resist the temptation of imitating the Egyptian custom of mummifying the bodies of the deceased and, no less, the practice of other neighbors who burned the remains of their dead. The "lofty" funeral pyre for Hector was meant to honor the hero of Troy (Iliad, XXIV, 782–804), while elsewhere cremation stemmed from a disdain for things physical. The Israelites, however, selected their burial sites with care. (Gn 23) They laid the dead bodies to rest fully clothed but without coffin, placing them in a niche or bed cut into the walls of a cave or in a tomb hewn out of soft rock so that dust would return to dust and bone lie next to bone. To be left unburied was considered a disgrace since it made the corpse an easy prey of vultures or wild beasts; worse, it was the most terrible curse, for the nefesh, "the soul," was held to feel whatever happened to sinews and bones. To bury the dead, however, was a work of piety, an evidence of "fearing" God, and a test of faith. (Tb 2,9; 12,12f)

Weeping for the deceased, bewailing their departure was never thought unmanly. (Gn 23,2; Sir 38,16) On the contrary, lamentations seem to have formed the substance of the funeral ceremony. They ranged from the simple "Alas! Alas!" (Am 5,16) or "Alas! alas! my brother" (1 Kgs 13,30) to David's heartrending cry: "My son Absalom! My son! My son Absalom! Would I had died in your place! Absalom my son! My son!" (2 Sm 19,1) and his elaborate dirge over Saul and Jonathan in which he recalls his happy love for Jonathan, his brother by choice—a friendship more marvelous than the love of women—and praises him and his father as having been swifter than eagles and stronger than lions. (2 Sm 1,26.23) Deeply moving though these laments are, they are expressions of strong human emotion rather than of religious faith. Still, they went hand in hand with penitential rites like fasting and the wearing of sackcloth, all of them signs of mourning, all of them duties to be paid to the deceased. The dead, then, continued to exist, though their existence could hardly be called "life." Were they not cut off from the community of the living on earth, indeed— such was Israel's fear for centuries—from the living God himself?

One must ask again: What was it that made the ancient Hebrews hold on to views of a fate as empty and bleak as these? It could not have been that, in their "stiff-necked" way (Ex 32,9), they defied a spiritual vision of the afterlife. Some writers have offered this solution while others have attributed the stagnation of this one segment of belief—a stagnation that prevails through most of the Old Testament—to Jewish "materialism." It is true, the Hebrews of old had a loving eye for the bounty of God's creation (Ps 148; Dn 3,52–90) and the marvel of life but this appreciation was spiritual, not materialistic. God's gift, life, was pleasing to him only when based on tsedakah, "right doing," they held. Their frequent resistance to God's will would never have stood in the way of a happier outlook on the individual's final destiny. Had they in fact been as materialistic as some self-righteous, censorious Christians thought them to have been, they would have been impelled to adopt the Egyptian or other phantasies.

95

As it is, they were solemnly warned against the abhorrent practices of their neighbors:

> When you come into the land which the Lord, your God, is giving you, you shall not learn to imitate the abominations of the peoples there. Let there not be found among you anyone who immolates his son or daughter in the fire, nor a fortuneteller, soothsayer, charmer, diviner, or caster of spells, nor one who consults ghosts and spirits or seeks oracles from the dead. Anyone who does such things is an abomination to the Lord. (Dt 18,9–12)

This prohibition is clear enough. The Israelites were to have no part in the kind of belief in man's survival that was common among Chanaanites and other peoples. To inquire of the dead, to benefit from any special knowledge they might have was the same as to run after sorcerers. Isaia derides necromancers, mediums, and fortunetellers as creatures who chirp and gibber. (Is 8,19) Israel must have recourse to the Holy One, not to mortals. Saul's shattering experience with the witch of Endor points in the same direction. When God no longer guided him, either through prophets or dreams, the lonely king turned to a woman with a crystal ball so that, for his inner comfort, she might bring up Samuel from the abode of the dead. When the woman, who well knew that her incantations were nothing but fraud, really saw an old man wrapped in a prophet's mantle, she shrieked. The king, however, heard Samuel castigate him for depending on "black art," even predict death and defeat: "Tomorrow you and your sons will be with me." (1 Sm 28,6–19)

The Deuteronomic injunction, Isaia's parody, and Saul's panic—all tell the same story: Survival after death was taken for granted but the Lord's hand kept Israel from interpreting it in pagan terms, from mistaking fancy for truth. Her neighbors' views would have drawn Israel away from simple obedience and untarnished service of God into a world of glittering magic and morbid sensuousness. In isolating her from the lure and fog of paganism, the Lord let her pass through what mystics call "the dark night of the soul." Only after centuries of inner suffering and deprivation, did Israel become ready for a fuller understanding of the life-to-come. To compare the past with the present: Not till the Christian world had witnessed the tears and blood of our century, did it come to a complete realization of every man's dignity, whatever his faith, whatever his conviction, whatever the shade of his skin. In fact, the knowledge of every man's worth has still not penetrated the curtain many Christians have hung around their hearts. Similarly, God's providence made the chosen people wait a millennium or more in order to learn that no power, not even death, can separate the *chasid*, the faithful one, from his Lord. (Ps 15[16]10)

THE TYRANNY OF DEATH   "We must all die, we are as water poured on the ground no one can gather up again." (2 Sm 14,14) These are words a woman from Tekoa addressed to David; many of her fellow Israelites, then and later, could have spoken thus, though they were by no means a morose, a dispirited people. Death is the fate common to all men. "Remember that death does not tarry," warns the sage. (Sir 14,12) For one it came yesterday, for another it will come today. (Sir 38,22) Biblical man neither rebelled against its universal rule, hard as it was to bear, nor did he divinize it, even though a divine decree had established its embrace of all flesh:

> O death! how bitter the thought of you . . .
> for the man unruffled and always successful. . . .
> O death! how welcome your sentence
> to the weak man of failing strength.
>
> (Sir 41,1–4)

Whether a man sits on a lofty throne or is wrapped in the coarsest of cloaks, the terror of death is always with him, its fear never far from his heart:

> A great anxiety has God allotted,
> and a heavy yoke, to the sons of men.
>
> (Sir 40,1–5)

For Scripture, death is not a mere biological phenomenon. Far from being part of God's original plan for man (Gn 2,17), it entered the world through "the envy of the devil" (Wis 2,24) and through man's ambition to be god-like in power though not in love. (Gn 3,4ff.19) Death is two-faced: on the one hand, God's appointee, on the other, an alien, a destroyer, a slayer, even an enemy. (Ex 12,23; 2 Kgs 19,35; 1 Cor 15,26)

In the Pentateuch and in other books of the Old Testament, the death-event is often called "to go to one's father," "to be gathered to one's kin," "to rest, to lie down with one's fathers." (Gn 15,15; 25,8; 47,30) These idioms are more than circumlocutions, more than euphemisms for the starkness of death. They imply more than interment in a family tomb. Though Abraham was not buried with his ancestors, God's voice had told him: "You shall go to your fathers in peace." (Gn 15,15) Rather do these expressions imply that the bond of kinship outlasts the hour of death: The dead man joins his people in "Sheol."

THE OPPRESSIVENESS OF THE NETHERWORLD   The etymology of Sheol is uncertain; among other things, it might mean "place of rest," "abode of the powerless," "the hollow deep down in the earth," or "the netherworld." One of its synonyms is "the pit," another is *abaddon*, "[the place of] destruction," that is, the place where man "perishes," where he can no longer do the things he did in the land of the living. With an imaginative power that knew little inhibition, the sacred writers compared the netherworld to a city whose gates once shut do not open; to an immense cemetery, with grave bordering on grave; to a voracious beast whose never closing jaws gulp the unexpected and bring low the haughty.[1] A "dark abyss," a "land of darkness and of gloom," a "disordered land where darkness is the only light"—such was the abode of the dead to the ancient Hebrews. (Ps 87[88]7; Jb 10,21f)

The inhabitants of the netherworld were sometimes called *refaim*, "the enfeebled ones," men and women who are "sunk," who have lost their energy and

97

---

[1] Is 38,10; Jon 2,7; Ez 32,17–32; Is 5,14; Hb 2,5; Prv 27,20.

grown slack. They were said to doze forever and ever. (Ps 12[13]4) Israel's formative spiritual experience was God's intervention in her history. His great and awesome deeds in her behalf—and *his* alone—made her discover history as a continuum of meaningful events. What to others was a series of disconnected happenings was revealed to her as a wondrous march toward a God-set destiny. The dead, however, were thought to have no part in the movement of history: They were sleepers. As if this were not enough, the inhabitants of Sheol were reduced to indistinction, to the lowest common denominator. Kings were lords of nothing but ruins, princes as poor as their neighbors, the wicked no longer troublesome, the weary at rest, prisoners at ease, and slaves "free." (Jb 3,14–19)

Deprived of their flesh, blood, and senses, the dead were regarded as being in a state of inaction. "There will be no work, nor reason, nor knowledge, nor wisdom in the netherworld," the Preacher despairs. (Coh 9,10) Gone from them will be the memory of the past; gone all love and hatred; never again will they "have part in anything that is done under the sun." (Coh 9,5f) A father will remain unaware of his sons' honors or their disgrace. (Jb 14,21) Unremembered by men, these shadows of their former selves will be forsaken by God, too, "cut off from [his] care." (Ps 30[31]13; Sir 38,21; Ps 87[88]6) Worse, these "weaklings" will not be able to rise either to give thanks to the Lord or to tell of his love and fidelity, much less to make known his wonders and justice in the land of silence and oblivion. (Ps 87[88]11ff) When psalmist, prophet, and preacher dwell on the inarticulateness of the dead, they have, above all, Israel's liturgy in mind. The hours in which the community assembled for the public praise of God, for its corporate worship and witness were its noblest and most spiritual; not to be able to join in them, was to the living an unspeakable loss.

FIRST SIGNS OF HOPE　One must not take all the statements on the fate of the dead literally. Biblical Hebrew uses few "ifs," "buts," or "thoughs"; it is always bold, trying to seize the complexity of things by means of sharp contrast. Neither classifying thoughts nor numbering them "first," "second," "third," and so on, it is spontaneous, even explosive. When happy, Hebrew men clap their hands and see the mountains leap; when sad, they cry out in pain while the world around them seems plunged into darkness. Some utterances deny to the departed all perception, but the frequent attempts to communicate with them and obtain their counsel show that the people, at least, assumed their superior understanding. While some passages suppose that the dead are dulled, Job spoke of the "powerless" beneath the earth as "writhing in terror" at the thought of God. (Jb 26,5) One psalmist declared that God works no wonders for the dead, that he has withdrawn from them his sustaining hand. (Ps 87[88]11.6) Another, however, rejoiced in the wonderful knowledge that, no matter how he tried, he could not flee God's all-piercing eye: Even if he made his bed in the netherworld, the Lord would be there, the Lord for whom "darkness itself is not dark, and night shines as the day." (Ps 138[139]7–12)

98　　Nothing can hide Sheol from God's sight: "Naked before him is the netherworld, coverless the realm of the dead." (Jb 26,6; cf. Prv 15,11.) Long before these words were written—a little less than 800 years prior to Christ—the prophet Amos had spoken in a similar vein. Announcing God's wrath over the people, he proclaimed that nothing would stand in the way of his judgment. Even if the guilty, fleeing from his sight, should break into the netherworld, the Lord's strong hand would take them out. (Am 9,2) Dire though his warning is, it clearly shows God's might to be greater than that of "the pit." Yahweh is the Lord of life and death:

> It is I who bring both death and life,
> I who inflict wounds and heal them.
> (Dt 32,39; cf. 1 Sm 2,6.)

He is the Master of the heavens and the earth. Is he, then, not also Master of the city of the dead? There would have been hardly anyone in Israel to deny his unbounded worship, yet it took time—that creative gift of the Creator—to draw from it the jubilant conclusion that illumines the "great Isaian Apocalypse." (Is 24–27)

Various dates have been assigned to this probably youngest part of the book of Isaia. Some exegetes think it was composed in the fifth century, others much later. If the earlier date is correct, then the oracle that on the great day-to-come the Lord would "destroy death forever . . . [and] wipe away tears from all faces" (Is 25,8) would be the earliest witness in Israel to the hope of sharing his glory. (Cf. 1 Cor 15,26.54.) This conquest of death will be the seal with which the Lord confirms a new community that unites Jews and gentiles with him. (Is 25,6f) Isaia's "great Apocalypse" contains another exultant oracle. Of the men slain in battle with God's enemies—enemies that fail to see his majesty and uplifted hand (Is 26,10f)—it proclaims:

> Your dead [O Lord] shall live, their corpses shall rise;
> awake and sing, you who lie in the dust.
> For your dew [O Lord] is a dew of light,
> and the land of shades gives birth.
> (Is 26,19)

Many exegetes consider this saying but a prediction of Israel's national and spiritual revival, while others give it the full force of a literal interpretation. Metaphor or reality, the rise of the "dust dwellers," the inhabitants of the grave, is a sign of dawning hope.

Yet, at the beginning of the fifth century, one of Israel's great thinkers and poets could not see beyond Sheol:

> For a tree there is hope,
> if it be cut down, that it will sprout again
> and that its tender shoots will not cease. . . .
> But when a man dies, all vigor leaves him;
> when a man expires, where then is he? . . .
> Men lie down and do not rise again.
> Till the heavens are no more, they shall not awake,
> nor be roused out of their sleep.
> (Jb 14,7.10.12)

99

Strangely enough, about the same time that the author of Job composed these lines of resignation, or possibly before, an old narrative of Henoch's "translation" into paradise was at last recorded. Still earlier, some time before the Babylonian exile, the stories of Elia, which must have been recited among the people from the eighth or ninth century B.C. on, were given their final and written form. One of them was the wonder of the prophet's assumption. To return to Henoch, of him it is said that, after he had ceaselessly "walked with God" among men, "he was seen no more because God took him." (Gn 5,24) In the words of the book of Wisdom, he was loved by God because of a life perfect and pleasing, and was thus "snatched away." The Lord himself "sped him out of the midst of wickedness" (Wis 4,10–14) and carried him to another life, to a divine reserve, because he believed. (Heb 11,5)

Of Elia, too, the people believed and Scripture relates that, enveloped in a whirlwind, he went up to heaven. A radiant cloud is said to have awaited him— in the figurative language of Scripture, a flaming wagon drawn by fiery horses. (2 Kgs 2,11) In the midst of a great apostasy, he was Yahweh's champion, the ever-forward-spurring leader of Israel's remnant. In order to prove to the shifting multitude that the alien gods of Chanaan were impotent, he offered sacrifice, praying: "Lord, God of Abraham, Isaac, and Jacob, let it be known that you are Israel's God, and I your servant," and the Lord heard him. He rallied the people, who had fallen on their faces in terror, to the acknowledgment that Yahweh was God: he alone. (1 Kgs 18,36.39) Had it not been for his zeal, there might have been no elite for the Lord to spare—no seven thousand men whose knees had not bent to *baal*, whose mouths had not kissed him. (1 Kgs 19,18) Hence, at the moment of their parting, his disciple Elisha thought him mightier than a whole army and cried out: "Israel's chariot and charioteers." (2 Kgs 2,12) No wonder, Israel was sure that the Lord would not permit so devoted a servant to descend into the netherworld but had made him mount to everlasting nearness.

Read as isolated texts, Job's complaint and the account of the glorious ascents of Henoch and Elia contradict one another: there, man's defeat by death; here, God's conquest of it. Seen in the ensemble of Holy Scripture, the three accounts are but signs of light's struggle to break through a dark cloud. The patriarch and the prophet were the first rays of Easter morning. They were the upcoming glimmer of dawn, of a dawn continuously threatened by the misery of death and of the life-to-come.

THE HEART'S DESIRE FOR LASTING UNION   Once that primitive optimism which expects to see the just rewarded and the wicked punished here and now had passed, Israel—in her *chasidim*, her faithful ones [2]—was plagued by the injustice of this world. Hence the singer's admonition not to be vexed over wrongdoers, nor to be jealous of them, rather to trust in the Lord and do good. Committing one's way to him, leaving things in

---

[2] In speaking of *chasidim*, the writer of this book does not wish to subscribe to the views of some scholars who seek the authors of certain psalms among a party of *chasidim*, living close to the Christian era. Throughout Israel's history, there have been several more or less organized groups of *chasidim*. Here, however, the term refers simply to the best in Israel. No secular society can flourish without an elite, much less can a spiritual community. Long before the prophets spoke of the remnant of Israel, her holy nucleus was her most responsive and active portion, the true bearer of saving history. *Chasid*, then, is the title of the true Israelite, of the one who lives the covenant, be he prophet, singer, or hidden saint.

his care and trust—such was the attitude the psalmist wished to instill in his fellows. (Ps 36[37]1–7)

> Yet a little while, and the wicked man shall be no more. . . .
> But the meek shall possess the land,
>   they shall delight in abounding peace.
>   (Ps 36[37]10f)

The psalmist did not know when and how this would happen, he only knew that the Lord's day was coming. (Ps 36[37]13) It is all the more marvelous that in spite of their dimmed vision, the saints of the Ancient Dispensation remained true to God's will.

The *chasidim* were men tied to God by *chesed,* by the offer of his covenant love and their response to it. They were men who lived in constant communion with him. It would be astonishing had they not longed to see their fellowship endure forever. Thus one *chasid,* embittered by the prosperity and arrogance of sinners, unsparingly accused himself of having been "like a brute beast in [God's] presence," only to go on:

> Yet with you I shall always be;
>   you have grasped my right hand. . . .
> Whom else have I in heaven?
>   When I am with you, the earth delights me not.
> Though my flesh and my heart waste away,
>   God is the rock of my heart and my portion forever.
>   (Ps 72[73]22–26)

The biblical "forever" does not always mean "through all eternity"; quite often it stands for "as long as I live." This could have been the intent of the psalmist's humble yet happy confession. But would such short-lived intimacy do justice to his prayer, to his faith in the all-conquering presence of the Lord? Though his deeply felt words may not have been a precise, unmistakable affirmation of everlasting life, they called for a fulfillment of his union, even after his strength was gone and his heart had failed. What the things-to-come would be like was hidden from him; still, the hidden God himself, not the poet's own emotion, was the Guarantor of never-ending love. The psalmist was truly one of God's children, imbued with the freedom that is theirs. Desiring no earthly reward, nothing but God himself, he was sure that to be with God is to live, while to be without him is to be dead even when apparently alive:

> As for me, to be near God is my happiness.
> I have made the Lord my refuge.
>   (Ps 72[73]28)

Another psalmist had been troubled by the haughtiness and the abuses of the rich but overcame his fear of their power, his envy of their splendor. He knew that none can avoid meeting death, the great leveler. His gladness, however, was not in the certitude that death would make an end to the boasting of those "knaves" and herd them like sheep into the nether-world, rather in the firm hope that God would "ransom," redeem him from the power of Sheol. More than this, God would receive him. (Ps 48[49]16) He was content to leave the future in the Lord's hands; death no longer frightened him. Though man was helpless in the face of death, God was not. Is it really enough to think, as some interpreters do, that all the psalmist hoped for was that God would spare him the calamity of a premature death? Is it not a much more adequate understanding of his words that, by God's grace, he hoped to pass through death as through a door and to enter into a union with God more intimate and blessed than the present one?

One more glance at the blossoming faith among the singers of Israel. The poet of Psalm 15[16] was one of those rare men of prayer who had never suffered hardship. His life was one of favors and hence of gratitude. So greatly blessed was he that he could say: "My Lord are you. Apart from you I have no good," no happiness. (Ps 15[16]2) So strong was his trust, so sure was he of the Lord's love that he could rejoice:

> You will not abandon my soul to the netherworld,
>   nor will you suffer your faithful one to undergo corruption.
> You will show me the path to life,
>   fullness of joys in your presence,
>   the delights at your right hand forever.
>
> (Ps 15[16]10f)

Here, too, a number of exegetes have tried to interpret this outburst of confidence as the psalmist's surety that God would save him from an early and unforeseen death but such an explanation reads thoughts into the text that are not there. No, the presence of the Lord who was ever before and ever with him begot in his heart the unshakable conviction that death was conquered and that life in God's presence would never end. The psalmist may not have realized that the outpourings of his heart were echoed in heaven. In any case, no sooner had he uttered his prayer, than it became that of Another. Thus the apostles saw in his certitude words spoken, as it were, by Jesus; words that revealed their fullest meaning only in his resurrection. (Ac 2,25–32; 13,35ff) Not subject to "corruption," no slave of dust, he rose to joy and glory.

THE FINAL BREAKTHROUGH   "There is an appointed time for every-thing . . . a time to be born, and a time to die; a time to plant, and a time to uproot the plant; a time to kill, and a time to heal," wrote the gloom-iest of sages. (Coh 3,1ff) "There is an allotted time for every activity here beneath the heavens" means that the right time for all things is limited and circumscribed. Everything grows and declines, begins and ends. God alone is without beginning and end. It was the constant fear of Israel's watchmen, her prophets and teachers, that God be drawn into the cycle of seasons; that he be made, not Master but part of nature; that he be conceived in the manner of the Chanaanite vegetation gods—gods who died and rose, fall after fall, spring after spring. This fear was among the causes of Israel's slowness, of the restraint that held down her hope of resurrection.

Finally, hope broke into the open. No longer were there but flashes like the assumptions of love by her *chasidim*—of a love that by its very nature demanded perpetuity, and of a union with God that contained within itself the seed of eternity. About 165 years before Christ's coming, the writer of the book of Daniel spoke out in indisputable terms. In a vision, he saw Israel's deliverance, the salvation of every one whose name is inscribed in the book of God's loving predestination. He saw, above all, the great rising that will take place on the day set by the Lord:

> Many of those who sleep
> in the dust of the earth shall awake;
> Some shall live forever,
> others shall be an everlasting horror and disgrace.
> But the wise shall shine brightly
> like the splendor of the firmament,
> And those who lead the many to justice
> shall be like the stars forever.
>
> (Dn 12,2f)

This promise explains itself. Though in the context in which it is given, it concerns only the Jewish people, the gentiles are not excluded from God's design. Resurrection—as will become abundantly clear at a still later stage of God's revelation—is all-embracing. The "many" in Daniel's apocalyptic vision are again "all," the doers as well as the mockers of his will. The first shall rise to never-ending love, the second to loneliness. Sin will be shamed and goodness triumph. Indeed, the more self-effacing the service of the just man, the higher his bliss.

The witness of the book of Daniel is surpassed by that of the second book of Machabees, written over a century before Jesus' birth. Its author, intent upon stirring the emotions of his readers rather than on simply narrating facts, tells of the glorious martyrdom of seven brothers and their mother under Antiochus Epiphanes, King of Syria. In order to assure his dominion over the Jews, the king had used every means to make them abandon fidelity to the God of Israel and his Law for the sake of Greek ways. In their agonized conscience, the Machabees resisted this attempt at spiritual subjugation. Because the second book of Machabees is filled with pathos, one scholar or another assumes that the account of the martyrdom of the seven and their mother is fictional: a tale invented by the writer to bring comfort and encouragement to his readers and to urge their perseverance in the ways of God.

Since the Christian faith in no way depends on the historicity of the story, as it does, for instance, on that of the crucifixion and resurrection of Jesus, it matters little whether or not the cruel tortures happened exactly as they are described. One may even venture to say: If the test and triumph of the Machabean martyrs is a factual report, it shines indeed with their splendor but is possibly the witness of only an elite. If the breathless drama is, however, an edifying composition written to exalt God's power, it voices certainly the author's belief in the resurrection and probably the hope of a multitude of readers, too. In either case, the faith the story proclaims stands firm.

When the first of the brothers was maltreated and put to death with unspeakable cruelty, the rest heartened one another with the assurance that God would not fail his servants but take pity on them. (2 Mc 7,3–6) Before breathing his last, the second brother told his tormentor, the king: "You wretch, you rob us of this present life but the King of the universe, for whose laws we die, will raise us up to everlasting life." (2 Mc 7,9) The third offered his tongue and hands to the king's henchmen: "These limbs are heaven's gift but for the sake of God's law I regard them as if they were nothing. From him do I hope to receive them again." (2 Mc 7,11) No less brave, the fourth of the brothers died with this certainty on his lips: "Better to die by the hands of men in the God-given hope to be raised anew. For you, however," he warned the king, "there will be no resurrection to life." (2 Mc 7,14) With like fortitude, the other brothers gave their bodies to be martyred.

Despite the manliness of the seven, the story is not meant to hail physical courage but to broadcast unbounded hope in the Lord. This is how the valiant mother is said to have encouraged her sons:

> I do not know how you were formed in my womb. For it was not I who gave you breath and life, not I who brought into harmony the limbs of every one of you. The Creator of the universe effects the birth of man and presides over the origin of all things. He, in his mercy, will restore to you breath and life. . . . (2 Mc 7,22f)

Bending down to her youngest child, she pleaded:

> My son, have pity on me! . . . I beg you, my child, look up at the heaven and the earth and all they contain; remember that God made them and humanity, too—out of nothing. Do not fear this butcher but show yourself worthy of your brothers in accepting death so that with them I may find you again, in the time of mercy. (2 Mc 7,27ff)

Fearlessly, the child laid down his life so that God's anger at Israel's sin might be appeased and his favor shine once more on his people. (2 Mc 7,37)

One can but repeat, historical figures or creations of a poet-preacher, the seven sons and their unique mother are gospellers before the advent of the Messia. They bear testimony to the faith of the greater part of Israel in the resurrection of the flesh and in the life-to-come [3]—a mystery that will be the heart of the gospel of Jesus the Christ.

The testimony of the seven is borne out later in the book by Juda the Machabean who is reported to have had a sacrifice offered in the Temple in order to expiate the sins of those slain in battle. His intercession is praised as a "very good and noble act because he kept in mind the resurrection." (2 Mc 12,43) It is sometimes claimed that Israel's hope of resurrection grew out of her meeting with Greek culture, or the religion of Zarathustra, or the myths and cults of gods that died and rose again. Quite apart from the fact that through the Old Testament runs an ever-renewed break with, even a declaration of war on, all mythology, the foreign ideas Israel encountered in those days served at the most as a catalyst. For the doctrine of the resurrection is an authentic fruit, indeed, the consummation of Israel's belief in the living God, mighty and just, who created the world in his goodness, made man a union of "body" and "soul," granting his favorite creature the grace of communion with him: a fellowship of love.

Finally, the book of Wisdom, youngest of Old Testament writings, looks toward a blessed life of the just, toward their receiving "from the hand of the Lord the crown of glory and the diadem of beauty." (Wis 5,16) The hope of resurrection, though not expressly stated, is no doubt implicit in its assurance of the faithful's share in God's eternity. The author was faced with pleasure lovers who took for their motto words like these: Brief is man's span, his breath but smoke, his life like a cloud speeding away. There is no remedy against death, let us therefore "enjoy the good things that are real," let us wade in costly wines and perfumes.

> Let us oppress the needy just man;
> let us neither spare the widow. . . .
> But let our strength be our norm of justice;
> for weakness proves itself worthless.
> (Wis 2,10f)

---

[3] Lest someone think that these professions of faith were rare instances without echo among the people, a few references to at least one of Israel's apocalyptic writings may be in order. Not included in the Canon of Scripture, they are called "apocryphal," that is, of doubtful authority. This is not the place, however, to discuss either the Apocrypha themselves, or their worth, or even some of their questionable statements. Widely read in their day, they must have reflected the mood, indeed, the hope of the devout. The book Henoch, for instance, probably written over a long period by several authors before and after the Machabean revolt from 166 to 134 B.C., gives this vision of messianic times: Once the Holy Great One has come forth from his dwelling and trod upon the earth, he will make peace with the righteous, protect the elect, and show them his mercy. They will all belong to him and be blessed. (Hen 1,3f.8) Those who had not been steadfast in obeying the commandments will find no peace. (5,4) Again, the sinners will be judged and driven from the face of the earth, while the just, without number, will be in the presence of God forever and ever. Thus they will be "as fiery lights . . . and their lips will extol the name of the Lord of spirits." (38,1; 39,6f) When the Son of Man will appear in his glory and might "the earth will give back that which has been entrusted to it, and Sheol also shall give back that which it owes." (48,2; 49,2; 51,1)

Men as base as these, he countered, were blinded by their wickedness, were unaware of "the hidden counsels of God" who made man imperishable, the image of his nature and endless being. (Wis 2,21ff)

> The souls of the just are in the hand of God,
> and no torment shall touch them.
>
> (Wis 3,1)

They are in peace. Not so the lot of the wicked; their hope is "like fine, tempest-driven foam, like smoke scattered by the wind." (Wis 5,14) Later the Apocalypse will call their fate "the second death," the mute company of hell.

> But the just shall live forever,
> and in the Lord is their recompense,
> and the thought of them is with the Most High. . . .
> For he shall shelter them with his right hand,
> and protect them with his arm.
>
> (Wis 5,15f)

In the books of Daniel, Machabees, and Wisdom, Israel's standstill became a leap *toward* the highest hope. The stage was set for him who could proclaim:

> I am the resurrection and the life;
> he who believes in me, even if he die, shall live;
> and whoever lives and believes in me, shall never die.
>
> (Jn 11,25f)

Jesus the Christ not only claimed power to give new life to others, but went himself from death to life: Out of the tomb his body rose, flooded by the Spirit, radiant, "winged," and thus free from every burden, every pain. Here as elsewhere, Christ is the Answer to questions the Old Testament had to leave open. In Tertullian's words, he is *Illuminator antiquitatum* (*Against Marcion*, IV,40), the One who casts light on the things of old, who makes clear the road the ancient Israel had to travel. Israel, it seems, had to wait for his rising to have the pall that had lain upon her for so long *fully* lifted because her faith was bound to the history of salvation. As Israel's exodus was necessary to beget the people's faith in the living God, so Christ's final exodus, his redeeming death and ascent to the Father, was needed for man's mature hope in everlasting life. Everlasting life is not the mere continuation of this life that is the philosophers' reasoned expectation, nor is it a natural transformation like that of the caterpillar into the butterfly—it is the overflow of God's love, man's admission to divine glory.

THE DAY OF YAHWEH

With sympathetic insight, the French scholar Edmond Jacob states that "the divine presence in the Old Testament may be defined as the presence of the God who comes." (*Theology of the Old Testament* [London: Hodder and Stoughton, 1955], p. 317) Deep though his observation is, it is one-sided. Scripture is quite definite on the Lord's dwelling with his people. A cloud, we are told, sign of his pervading presence, hovered over the Tent of Meeting, Israel's first sanctuary. (Ex 40,36ff) According to one of Isaia's visions, the "train of his garment" filled the Temple. (Is 6,1) Solemnly, the impassioned Lord declared that he *was* in Israel's midst. (Dt 6,15) Still, he came, comes, and will come to intervene on her, but also on the nations' behalf. He comes in order to judge and to save.

All through its history, the chosen people was engaged in battles with its neighbors or drawn into the wars the great powers waged against each other. Whenever this happened, the people's existence was endangered, its sovereignty and nationhood threatened; worse, its heritage—the burden of faith, worship, and virtue the Lord had placed on its shoulders—was at stake. Thus Israel thought of her wars as holy wars but, at the same time, dreamt with Isaia of peace, of the never-ending peace of messianic times:

> Then the wolf shall be a guest of the lamb,
>   and the leopard shall lie down with the kid;
> The calf and the young lion shall browse together,
>   with a little child to guide them.
>
> (Is 11,6)

PAST AND FUTURE VICTORIES   In Israel's early days, every victory was considered a day of Yahweh; in the prophetic era, however, "Day of Yahweh" pointed toward the future. So common was its expectation that it was sometimes referred to as "that day" or simply "the day." The great day of the Lord's final intervention that would bring about the triumph of his justice might not break till far-off times; at least, the complacent and overconfident were tempted to put off what they called "the evil day." (Am 6,1.3) But the prophets—in a holy eagerness and with that telescoping sense of time which blends events close and distant, a sense of time that brings into one today, tomorrow, and the end of history—frequently see the day at hand. "Howl, for the day of the Lord is near," Isaia clamors. (Is 13,6) "In a little while," Osea announces in Yahweh's name, "I will punish." (Os 1,4) On the other hand, Isaia proclaims:

> But a very little while,
>   and Lebanon shall be changed into an orchard. . . .
> On that day the deaf shall hear . . . ,
>   the eyes of the blind shall see.
> The lowly will ever find joy in the Lord,
>   and the poor rejoice in the Holy One of Israel.
>
> (Is 29,17ff)

At all times, the heralding of "the day" was part of the prophets' demand for penance as well as their offer of consolation; before the exile, the first prevailed over the other, while during Israel's misery the men of God became her comforters. Judgment and salvation were the two great themes of their proclamation because they are the strong arms with which the Lord will establish his everlasting, never-to-be-challenged reign.

JUDGMENT   The book of Amos announces that "the Lord will roar from Sion" because of the numberless crimes of the nations and of his own people. (Am 1,2–2,16) The catalogue of their sins fills utterance after utterance, only to culminate in a threefold "Woe!"

> Woe to those who turn judgment to wormwood
>   and cast justice to the ground. . . .
> Woe to those who yearn for the day of the Lord!
>   what will this day of the Lord mean for you?
> Darkness, and not light! . . .
> Woe to the complacent in Sion,
>   to the overconfident on the mount of Samaria. . . .
>   (Am 5,7.18; 6,1)

Other prophets warned:

> They have come, the days of punishment!
>   they have come, the days of recompense!
> Let Israel know it!
>   (Os 9,7)

> Thus says the Lord God: Disaster upon disaster!
> See it coming! . . . The end is coming upon you! . . .
>   (Ez 7,5f)

The days of punishment, the time of disaster, the hour that will turn vast lands into ruins, ashes, or deserts are often called "an end," "the end." (Ez 7,2.6) Punishment and disaster are called "end" because they announce that history is not a perpetual spinning wheel but a movement toward consummation. "The end" is not always the final end, however, from which no one can escape. "Yet even in those days, says the Lord, I will not wholly destroy you." (Jer 5,18) The fire raging through his vineyard (Jer 5,10–17), for instance—that is, Jerusalem's siege and destruction—is but an anticipation of the *éschata,* the last events. For the Christian, too, the present agonies and joys, events great and small, summon the future; indeed, every day carries within it the germ of the ultimate, the irrevocable day. All through this short span, then, the Christian already lives in eschatological time, in the "final days": Bringing sorrow *and* fulfillment, they reveal God's dominion.

"Darkness, not light" for the house of Israel—such will be the day of the Lord, Amos warned. (Am 5,18) "A day of clouds, doomsday for the nations shall it be," Ezechiel exhorted. (Ez 30,3) What a bitter experience: a day of wrath, of anguish and distress, of destruction and desolation! (So 1,15) "Blazing like an oven" will the day-to-come be. It will turn the arrogant and the wicked into stubble, set them on fire, "leaving them neither root nor branch." And the wicked "will become ashes . . . on the day I take action, says the Lord of hosts." (Mal 3,19) Before the executors of God's anger—the scourges he unleashed on Israel—the earth will tremble and the heavens shake, sun and moon will be darkened and the stars will withhold their brightness. (Jl 2,10) Panic will strike, men will hide in the dust from the dread presence of the Lord, or crawl into holes, and their hearts will melt in terror. (Is 2,10.19; 13,7) Yet, when God will send his messenger, his herald will be "like the refiner's fire." He will refine the people "like gold or like silver that they may offer due sacrifice to the Lord." (Mal 3,1ff; cf. Mt 11,10; 3,11ff.)

SALVATION   Judgment is not God's final word. His final word is the same as his first: love, salvation. Even a prophet like Amos, sent to denounce and indict, must eventually reveal Israel's restoration. (Am 9,14) Were the chosen people to set free the oppressed, share bread with the hungry, shelter the homeless, and clothe the naked, a light would break forth and the Lord would be with them as their Guide, their Strength, and their Delight. (Is 58,6–14; cf. Mt 25,34–40.) "The days are coming, says the Lord, when I will fulfill the promise I made to the house of Israel and Juda. In those days, in that time, I will raise up for David a just shoot [the Messia]; he shall do what is right and just in the land." So much so that "the Lord our justice" will be the watchword of the dwellers in the new Jerusalem, of all those who surrender to the great offspring of David. (Jer 33,14ff)

The Lord's justice—his faithfulness—is not restricted to Israel: "Many peoples and strong nations shall come to seek the Lord of hosts in Jerusalem and implore the favor of the Lord." (Za 8,22) It is the new Israel, an Israel filled with the Spirit, graced with a new heart that will be God's people forever: the salt of the earth, a lamp among the nations, in short, the soul of the world. (Mt 5,13–16) A child will be born—Israel's child, mankind's child, nay, God's son—the "Prince of peace [whose] dominion is vast and forever peaceful." (Is 9,5f) Yes, if Israel listens, if the nations hearken, peace will come like a mighty river (Is 48,18), all the earth will shout for joy, will sing to God and praise him forever: "How tremendous are your deeds!" (Ps 65[66]1ff) If those whom God addresses through his Messia fully respond, mankind will be transfigured and the world transformed.

> Lo, I am about to create new heavens
> and a new earth. . . .
> I create Jerusalem to be a joy
> and its people to be a delight.
>   (Is 65,17f; cf. Ap 21,1–4.)

109

The day of Yahweh is meant to be a crisis, the climax of history, the dividing line: a day that marks the end of the age of sin and the beginning of the age of justice, that is, of grace, of fidelity, of love. In the opinion of Edmond Jacob, the eschatological drama is best summed up in the Hebrew idiom *shub shebut,* usually rendered "the return of captives." According to him, it should rather be understood as "great restoration" or "turning point" in the destinies of man and cosmos. (Ps 125[126]4; cf. Ac 3,21. *Theology of the Old Testament,* p. 320) With the coming of Jesus the Messia, there came crisis, division, and change. Yet his advent was not the end of the world of sin, of dull hearts and ears deaf to the breathings of the Spirit. Had Israel's leaders not misdirected their people so as to make them stumble (Rom 11,11); had they not been blinded to the wonder of Jesus, his coming would have been the ultimate turning point in the history of salvation. He would have said then, at the fullness of time, for all to hear what he said in the solitude of Patmos and will shout again at the summit of the ages: "Behold, I make all things new! . . . It is done! I am the Alpha and the Omega, the beginning and the end. To him who thirsts I will give freely of the fountain of the water of life." (Ap 21,5f)

Though the whole of his people did not receive him, the Christ-event is nonetheless the "day of the Lord," his epiphany, his manifestation, the dawn and rising of the goodness of God our Savior, of his love for man. (Ti 3,4) It is the midpoint of redemptive history. A holy remnant, so often the bearer of God's saving promise, became the bridge to the nations, the nucleus of the all-embracing Israel. (Rom 9,27ff; Is 10,22; 1,9) Yet the many sons of Abraham's loins, still aloof from Christ, are not abandoned; with the apostle, the Church shares the anguish for their salvation. Though they were given the privileged title "Israelites," that is, men victoriously struggling with God (Gn 32,29) or men proclaiming his power and lordship; though they were made his sons; though the glory of the divine presence is theirs, as are the covenants, the worship, and the promises; though the Christ took flesh from them through Mary his mother, the vast majority of them are separated from him. (Rom 9,1–5) Thanks to God's enduring love and fidelity, the Church not only grieves like St. Paul, but also like him hopes for the day of their restoration, for the day on which the descendants of Abraham's loins and those of his spirit will be one. (Rom 11,11f.23.25f)

With the whole of creation, the Church groans and suffers the birth pangs of the ultimate fulfillment of God's promise. With the universe, she awaits in eager longing the day of the Lord when the freedom and splendor of God's children will be unveiled and blanket the earth. She looks ahead to the day on which hope will give way to reality. Yet, she not only groans, suffers, and waits; on every Sunday—each a "day of the Lord," each a little Easter—she tastes in advance the glory that is to come.

A Few Basic Books

*Anderson, B. W., *Understanding the Old Testament* (Englewood Cliffs, N.J.: Prentice-Hall, 1957).

Bouyer, L., *The Meaning of Sacred Scripture* (Notre Dame, Ind.: University of Notre Dame Press, 1958).

Charlier, C., *The Christian Approach to the Bible* (Westminster, Md.: Newman, 1958).

De Vaux, R., *Ancient Israel* (New York: McGraw-Hill, 1962).

Dougherty, J. J., *Searching the Scriptures* (Garden City, N.Y.: Hanover House, 1959).

*Eichrodt, W., *Theology of the Old Testament* (Philadelphia: Westminster, 1961).

Giblet, J., ed., *The God of Israel, the God of Christians* (New York: Desclee, 1961).

Grollenberg, L. H., *Atlas of the Bible* (New York: Nelson, 1956).

*Knight, G. A. F., *A Christian Theology of the Old Testament* (Richmond, Va.: John Knox, 1959).

*Köhler, L., *Hebrew Man* (Nashville: Abingdon, 1957).

McEleney, N. J., ed., *Pamphlet Bible Series* (New York: Paulist Press, 1959–63).

McKenzie, J. L., *The Two-Edged Sword* (Milwaukee: Bruce, 1956).

Murphy, R. E., *Seven Books of Wisdom* (Milwaukee: Bruce, 1960).

Oesterreicher, J. M., ed., *The Bridge* (New York: Herder and Herder, 1955–62), Vols. I–IV.

*Rowley, H. H., *The Faith of Israel* (Philadelphia: Westminster, 1957).

Sutcliffe, E. F., *The Old Testament and the Future Life* (Westminster, Md.: Newman, 1947).

Tresmontant, C., *A Study of Hebrew Thought* (New York: Desclee, 1960).

Vawter, B., *A Path Through Genesis* (New York: Sheed and Ward, 1956).

——, *The Conscience of Israel* (New York: Sheed and Ward, 1961).

*Von Rad, G., *Old Testament Theology* (New York: Harper, 1962).

*Vriezen, Th., *An Outline of Old Testament Theology* (Boston: Branford, 1958).

Books carrying an asterisk are by non-Catholic authors.
Books referred to in the text are not mentioned again.

ABBREVIATIONS

Old and New Testament Books Used in This Volume

Genesis	Gn	Canticle of Canticles	Ct
Exodus	Ex	Wisdom	Wis
Leviticus	Lv	Sirach (Ecclesiasticus)	Sir
Numbers	Nm	Isaia	Is
Deuteronomy	Dt	Jeremia	Jer
Joshua	Jos	Lamentations	Lam
Judges	Jgs	Baruch	Bar
Ruth	Ru	Ezechiel	Ez
1 Samuel (1 Kings)	1 Sm	Daniel	Dn
2 Samuel (2 Kings)	2 Sm	Osea	Os
1 Kings (3 Kings)	1 Kgs	Joel	Jl
2 Kings (4 Kings)	2 Kgs	Amos	Am
1 Chronicles (Paralipomenon)	1 Chr	Jona	Jon
2 Chronicles (Paralipomenon)	2 Chr	Michea	Mi
Ezra	Esd	Habacuc	Hb
Nehemia (2 Ezra)	Neh	Sophonia	So
Tobia	Tb	Zacharia	Za
Job	Jb	Malachia	Mal
Psalms	Ps(s)	1 Machabees	1 Mc
Proverbs	Prv	2 Machabees	2 Mc
Coheleth (Ecclesiastes)	Coh		

In the enumeration of the Psalms, the first number follows the Vulgate, the number within brackets, the Hebrew text.

The transliteration of Hebrew words deliberately avoids scientific symbols unknown to the general reader. English consonants and vowels, however, are not always the equivalents of their Hebrew counterparts. The Hebrew "ch," for instance, a guttural sound, is not to be pronounced like the "ch" in "chair" or in "ache."

St. Matthew	Mt	Philippians	Phil
St. Mark	Mk	Colossians	Col
St. Luke	Lk	1 Thessalonians	1 Thes
St. John	Jn	1 Timothy	1 Tm
Acts of the Apostles	Ac	Titus	Ti
Romans	Rom	Hebrews	Heb
1 Corinthians	1 Cor	St. James	Jas
2 Corinthians	2 Cor	1 St. Peter	1 Pt
Galatians	Gal	1 St. John	1 Jn
Ephesians	Eph	Apocalypse	Ap

Apocrypha and Other Source Material

The Apocalypse of Ezra	4 Esd	*Summa Theologiae*	
Henoch	Hen	S. Thomae Aquinatis	*S.Th.*
Denzinger-Schönmetzer, *Enchiridion*		*The Church Teaches*	
Symbolorum. . . , 32nd ed.		ed. J. Clarkson and others	*TCT*
[Handbook of Creeds. . . .]	D		

112

INDEX

A

Aaronic blessing, 50f
Abraham, 3f, 13, 14, 17, 25, 34, 41, 55, 76, 94, 97
  descendants of (see Israel, ancient)
  spiritual offspring of, 4f, 25, 55
Abraham's bosom, 4
Adam, 23, 25, 38
  sin of, 29-32
Ancient Dispensation (see Covenant, Old; Law, the)
Anthropomorphisms, 7-10, 14f
Apocrypha, 105n
Apostles, the, 19, 82-87, 91, 102
Aramaic, 16, 89f
Aristotle, 3
Ark of the Covenant, 56, 58, 64
Atonement, 43, 64n, 65f (see also Repentance)
  Day of, 34, 65
  prayers of, 35f, 70
Augustine, St., 60ff
Awe of God, 13, 52
Azazel, 66

B

Babel, 8, 55
Babylon
  myths of, 16
  view of death in, 94
Babylonian captivity, 41f, 64, 78f, 82, 99f
Baptism, 4, 68, 70f
  of proselytes, 70
Beasts, mythological, 17, 18
Bede, Venerable, 68
Bethlehem, 49
Billerbeck, Paul, 84f
Bishop, consecration of, 5, 70
Blood
  of Jesus, 55, 71, 90
  sacredness of, 10n, 27, 64n, 68
Burnt-offering, 64

C

Calendar, fixing of, 83ff
Canon of Scripture, 105n
Celibacy, 23
Cereal-offering, 64
Chanaanites, 14, 96, 103
Christ, the (see Jesus)
Church, the, 4f, 13, 19, 45, 46, 53, 54, 55, 59, 61, 67f, 69ff, 73n, 83, 89, 90, 92, 110
Circumcision, 68f, 77
Cities of refuge, 40
Cleanthes, 15
Communion of saints, 76
Condescension, law of, 48f
Conversion (see Repentance)
Council of Florence, 67
Council of Trent, 66, 67, 90n
Covenant, Book of the, 56
Covenant, nature of, 46f
Covenant, New, 5, 16, 23, 49, 50, 65, 66, 75f, 80, 90ff
  continuation of Old, 2-5, 13, 75
  promise of, 79f, 99
Covenant, Old, 46-49, 52, 53, 55ff, 65, 67, 76n, 79
  Abrahamitic, 3, 43, 48n
  Sinaitic, 48, 75, 80, 92
  breaking of, 21, 29, 32, 34, 53, 79f
  renewal of, 43, 48n, 73
Creation, 7, 16ff, 21

D

Dante, 3
David, 17, 29, 41, 47, 48n, 58, 80f, 95, 96, 109
Day of Yahweh, 78, 106-110
Death, 41, 92, 93-106

E

Easter, 100, 110
Easter vigil, 4, 37

Egypt
  belief in afterlife, 93ff
  circumcision in, 69
  death of firstborn in, 38f, 72
  Israel's sojourn in, 87f, 93f
Elia, 100
Erasmus of Rotterdam, 54n
Eucharist, the, 88-92
Evangelists, the, 81, 83-86
Evolution
  of cosmos, 16f
  of faith (see Revelation, progressive)
Exodus, the, 17f, 23, 72f, 106
Exodus theme, 78f
Exsultet, the, 37
Extreme Unction, 69
Ezra Apocalypse, 30

F

Faith, 3, 4, 13f, 28, 68, 75, 83, 94ff, 102, 104f, 106
Fire, 3, 48
Firstborn, ransom of the, 38f
Flesh, the, 19ff, 90
Flood, the, 9, 30, 70
Forgiveness (see Pardon)
Francis of Assisi, St., 70
Freedom
  of God, 33, 42, 54
  of Israel, 41
  of man, 27, 44f, 59, 86, 101, 110

G

Gelin, Albert, 23, 62
Gentiles, 5, 24, 99, 103
Ginzberg, Louis, 32
God
  Hope of Israel, 70
  the Pardoner, 34, 36f
  the Redeemer, 43f
God of Israel, 2-5, 6-16
  fidelity of, 3, 32, 36, 52, 73, 78, 79, 98, 109f
  gracious deeds of, 3f, 7, 17, 21, 39, 72, 75, 78, 98
  presence of, 4, 8, 15, 20, 58, 64f, 70, 78, 80, 101f, 107
  salvific will of, 17, 48f, 66, 68, 72
Golden calf, 32, 34, 56
Gospel of Jesus, 41, 71, 105
Grace, 24, 29, 32f, 35-38, 44f, 49-53, 54, 72, 76, 82, 102
  Christian teaching on, 50, 53, 67f
  and equity, 39
Gregory the Great, St., 68

Grelot, Pierre, 55
Guillet, Jacques, 11f, 49f
Guilt-offering, 65f

H

Haggadah, the, 75
Hallel, the, 86, 88, 91
Hammurabi, Code of, 40
Hebrew mentality, 7, 9f, 13-16, 19, 21, 23, 27f, 31, 42f, 51, 56, 59n, 64, 76n, 89f, 95, 98
Henoch, 99f
History, sacred (see Salvation, history of)
Holiness-Code, 56
Holy Orders, 70
Holy Spirit, 3, 50, 54, 57, 71, 91, 106, 109f
Hope, 35, 37, 78, 81, 82, 94f, 98-106, 110
Hugh of St. Victor, 66, 68
Hypostatic union, 90n

I

Ill, sacrament for the, 69
Images, man-made, 7, 22
Intercession, 34
Isaian Apocalypse, great, 99
Israel, ancient
  Abraham's descendants, 3, 43, 55, 68, 110
  call of, 13f, 17, 19, 81f, 107
  history of, 14, 19, 33, 49, 50, 57, 63f, 68, 70, 72, 75, 79, 82, 98, 100n, 107
  infidelities of, 8, 21, 31f, 34, 41ff, 51f, 53, 78, 79, 104
  neighbors of, 14, 16, 33, 40n, 47, 48, 54, 59, 71, 96
  paradigmatic people, 31, 36, 49
  people of God, 9, 11, 53-59, 103
  priestly role, 54f, 63-76
Israel, the new (see Church, the)

J

Jacob, Edmond, 106f, 110
Jaubert, Annie, 83
Jesus, 1, 4, 11, 16, 20, 21f, 23, 40, 52n, 55, 59n, 69f, 71, 75f, 78n, 79, 80, 81, 82-92, 110
  love of, 13, 23, 50, 86, 87
  the paschal Lamb, 73, 83, 85, 90
  and the psalms, 59-63

Jesus (Cont.):
  redemptive work of, 4, 13, 17, 18,
    33n, 38, 39, 43ff, 50, 57, 67, 71,
    81, 92, 106
  second coming of, 45, 79
  Servant of Yahweh, 19, 61, 66, 90
Jewish tradition, 58, 70, 83
Jews in Christian era, 5, 23, 24, 39, 43
John the Baptist, 3, 71
John the Evangelist, 44, 75, 83ff, 87
John XXIII, Pope, 51n
Jonathan, 33, 47, 95
Joseph, St., 60
Joseph in Egypt, 29
Josia, 48n, 64
Judaism, 38, 83
Judgment, 108f
Justification, 36, 69, 91
Just in Israel, the, 30

K

Knowledge, 21f, 80

L

Lagrange, M.-J., 84
Lamb, the paschal, 68, 71ff, 83-86, 88
Lamentations, 34, 58f, 95
Last supper, 81-92
Law, the, 21, 27f, 34, 38ff, 43, 50, 55ff,
    63-76, 77, 80, 83, 84f, 88, 96
  Decalogue, 3, 24, 56, 80, 85n
Laying on of hands, 65, 70
Leaven, 72f
Legalism, reproach of, 56, 76, 80
Life
  love of, 9f, 95
  sacredness of, 10n, 101
Liturgy
  of ancient Israel, 58f, 70, 74, 91, 98
  of the Church, 4f, 15, 36, 59, 80
Lord, the (see God; God of Israel)
Love
  God's initiative, 3, 9, 21, 41ff, 46,
    48f, 51, 98, 101, 106, 109f
  man's response, 56, 76, 80, 103
Lyonnet, Stanislas, 32

M

Macchabean martyrs, 103ff
Magisterium of the Church, 90n
Man, 16-25
  dignity of, 22, 96
  failure of, 9, 26f, 53, 79
  image of God, 21f, 26f

Marriage, 4, 69f
  of Jews, 23, 31, 69, 79
Mary, mother of Jesus, 21, 49, 60, 75,
    110
Mass, the, 4, 15, 24, 53, 66, 92
Master race, fallacy of, 48
Materialism, reproach of, 10n, 32n, 95
Mémorial, Pascal's, 2f
Merit, 24, 41, 49
Messia, the, 17, 70, 81, 104, 109f
Messianic age, 17, 70f, 105n, 107 (see
    also Reign of God)
Messianic banquet, 78, 82, 92
Messianic hope, 52, 68, 70, 77-81
Metonymy, 89n, 90
Michelangelo, 34n
Miserere, the, 30
Moderation, 40
Moral science, 27f
Moses, 3, 12f, 17, 20, 32, 34, 41, 48,
    50, 55, 72, 80, 94
Moses, Song of, 9, 15, 54f
Music, 4f, 58ff
Mystical body of Christ, 61, 71, 89, 92

N

Nathan, 29
Nations, the, 9, 24f, 54f, 110
Netherworld, 41, 97-100, 102
New Dispensation (see Covenant, New)
New Testament, 2-5, 16, 19, 33, 44f,
    55, 81, 83-86
Nisan, month of, 74, 83ff

O

Obedience, 55f
Old Testament
  heritage of Christians, 2-5, 15
  leading themes of, 91f
  no systematic distinctions in, 7, 53, 98
  total vision of, 17-25
  vehicle of revelation, 7f, 10, 14, 41,
    105
Ovid, 22

P

Pagan feasts, transformation of, 73n
Pagan myths and gods, 9, 10, 12, 14,
    16, 22, 47, 74, 79, 93-96, 100,
    103, 105
Parables of Jesus, 10, 78n
Parallelism, poetic, 56, 76n

Pardon, 32-37, 64n, 80
Pascal, Blaise, 1-5
Passover, the, 71f
    celebration of, 60, 72-76, 77, 82-88, 90, 92
    the new (Pasch), 81-92
Patriarchs, the, 3, 55, 75
Paul, St., 5, 20n, 23, 34, 38, 39, 44, 50, 54, 64f, 69f, 73, 76, 79, 80, 89, 92, 110
Peace-offering, 65
Penance, sacrament of, 29, 70
Penitential liturgies, 35f, 70
Penitential rites, 34, 95
Pentecost, 3, 68, 75, 91
    in Israel, 85
People of God (see Church, the; Israel, ancient)
Peter, St., 11, 21, 79
Petition, 72
Pharisees, 83, 84f
Philosophy, Western, 2f, 6f, 21
Plato, 2f, 19
Plautus, 54n
Poor in Israel, the, 49, 60
Poverty, voluntary, 10n, 22
Praise, hymns of, 58ff
Priesthood, the, 29, 54
    of Israel, 63-71
Priests in Israel, 65, 70, 84
Privilege, misuse of, 19, 48
Prophets, the, 15, 28, 29, 31, 33, 36, 42, 48, 52, 76, 78, 81, 100n, 102f, 107ff
Prosperity, 10n
Psalms, the, 17, 42f, 50, 57-62, 70, 91, 100ff
    curses in, 59
    and Jesus, 59-63

Q

Qumrân, community of, 22f, 70f, 83f

R

Rabbis of old, 32, 64n, 87
Ransom, 33, 37, 38f, 41
Redemption, 5, 20n, 37-45, 49, 75
Reign of God, 17, 58, 71, 73n, 81 (see also Messianic age)
Remnant in Israel, 50, 51, 60, 82, 100, 110
Repentance, 33-36, 71, 107 (see also Atonement)

Resurrection
    of Jesus, 50, 102, 104, 106
    of man, 20, 102-106
Revelation, 7f, 41, 54, 68, 103
    progressive, 13f, 16f, 59n
Ricciotti, Guiseppe, 85
Robinson, H. Wheeler, 23
Rowley, Harold H., 57

S

Sabbath, 84f
Sacraments, 4, 10, 67, 69f
    ancient, 66-76
Sacrifices, 34, 63-66 (see also Passover)
Sadducees, 84f
Salvation, 12, 17f, 68, 73n, 109f
    history of, 3f, 7, 16ff, 25, 32, 48n, 55, 68, 73, 75, 78f, 82, 83, 88, 98, 100n, 106, 108ff
Samuel, 96
Sanhedrin, 85
Saul, 33, 95, 96
Scapegoat, 34, 65
Science, 2f, 16f
Second Isaia, 17f, 37, 42, 57, 66, 78f
Seder, 75, 86ff
Segregation, 24f
Self-righteousness of Christians, 51n, 95
Septuagint, 82
Servant of Yahweh, 19, 24, 61, 66, 90
Servant Songs, 24
Service, 19, 28, 54, 74
Shekels, 39
Sheol, 41, 97ff, 102, 105n
Sin, 13, 26-32, 37f, 44, 55, 59n, 61, 70, 103, 110
    involuntary, 27f, 40, 65
    original, 24, 29-32, 68
Singularity
    of the Church, 19
    of Israel, 9, 14, 18f, 54f, 81f, 107
    of man, 18f, 21f
Sin-offering, 65
Slaves in Israel, 41
Snaith, Norman H., 49, 51
Sodom, 28f
Solidarity
    of community, 23ff, 39, 56, 68
    of generations, 23f, 74ff
    of God with man, 32, 52
    of mankind, 24f
    role in Catholic theology, 24, 92
    of sinners, 29-32
Solomon, 65
Soul, the, 20, 95
Stoic belief, 15

T

Talion, law of, 40
Temple, the, 58f, 64, 65, 74, 81, 83, 86, 105, 107
Tertullian, 106
Thanksgiving, 58f, 64, 72, 76, 83, 86, 88, 91, 102
Theologians
  ancient, 32, 72
  modern, 7, 83
Thomas Aquinas, St., 13n, 59n, 67f, 90n
Tithes, 66
Type, biblical, 70

U

Unleavened Bread, feast of, 72f, 83ff

V

Vengeance
  blood, 39f
  of God, 40
  prayers for, 59
Vindication, 39f

W

Washings, ritual, 70f
Word made flesh, the, 20, 67
Worship, 19, 47, 55, 58f, 63-76
Wright, G. Ernest, 14

Y

Yahweh, the divine name, 11f, 14

Hebrew, Greek, and Latin Words and Phrases

abaddon, 97
Abba, 16
afikoman, 87f
ahabah, 51f, 53
ahabat 'olam, 51
añawim, 60
ani Yahweh, 56
asham, 65f
asirey ha-tikvah, 94
avodah, 19
baal, 14, 100
basar, 20
berachah, 88
berit, 47
chaburah, chaburot, 83
chai Yahweh, 11
chanan, 50
charoset, 87
chasid, chasidim, 96, 100f, 103
chasidei Yahweh, 17
chatt'at, 65
chen, 50f, 53
chesed, 52f, 57, 76n, 101
Ecclesía toû Theoû, 54
ehyeh asher ehyeh, 12
El, Elohim, 14
El-olam, 14
El-shaddai, 14

Elohim hashibenu, 36
emet, 52
éschata, 108
ga'al, 38-41
go'el, 41-45
go'el ha-dam, 40
homo homini lupus, 54n
hýbris, 8, 55
Illuminator antiquitatum, 106
imitatio Dei, 57
iste cantator, 60f
kehal Yahweh, 54
kiddush, 86
kodesh [ha-] kodashim, 64
koinōnía, 92
korban, 64
leitourgía, 19
lex talionis, 40
magnalia Dei, 4
matsot, 72
mikweh, 70
minchah, 64
natalis invicti solis, 73n
nefesh, 30, 95
'olah, 64
padah, 38-41
pasach, 72
Pesach, 72

pidyon, 38
ra', 27
rachamim, 52
rechem, 52
refaim, 97
ruach, 20
shub, 33
shub shebut, 110
tehillim, 58

torah, 56, 80
tsedakah, 95
tsedikot Yahweh, 78
vi naturalis connexionis et concomitantiae, 90n
vi verborum, 90n
Yahweh Tseba'ot, 15
zebach shelamim, 65
zikkaron, 72, 92

Index prepared by Josephine D. Casgrain